Penguin Masterstudies

Absalom and Achitophel

Raman Selden was educated at University College, London and Birkbeck College. He has held teaching posts at Portsmouth Polytechnic and Durham University. He is now a Professor in the English Department at Lancaster University. His publications include *English Verse Satire 1590–1765* (1978), *Criticism and Objectivity* (1984) and *A Reader's Guide to Contemporary Literary Theory* (1985).

Penguin Masterstudies
Joint Advisory Editors:
Stephen Coote and Brian Loughrey

John Dryden

Absalom and Achitophel

Raman Selden

Penguin Books

Penguin Books Ltd, Harmondsworth, Middlesex, England
Viking Penguin Inc., 40 West 23rd Street, New York, New York 10010, U.S.A.
Penguin Books Australia Ltd, Ringwood, Victoria, Australia
Penguin Books Canada Limited, 2801 John Street, Markham, Ontario, Canada L3R 1B4
Penguin Books (N.Z.) Ltd, 182–190 Wairau Road, Auckland 10, New Zealand

First published 1986

Copyright © Raman Selden, 1986
All rights reserved

Made and printed in Great Britain by
Richard Clay (The Chaucer Press) Ltd, Bungay, Suffolk
Filmset in Monophoto Times

Except in the United States of America, this book is sold subject
to the conditon that it shall not, by way of trade or otherwise, be lent,
re-sold, hired out, or otherwise circulated without the
publisher's prior consent in any form of binding or cover other than
that in which it is published and without a similar condition
including this condition being imposed on the subsequent purchaser

To Harold Brooks

                . . . to whom I owe
All that I am in arts, all that I know
(How nothing's that!)

Contents

Introduction	9
1 Dryden's Life and Writings	11
2 *Absalom and Achitophel*: A Commentary on the Poem	15
The Immediate Political Context	
The Poem's Structure	
A Commentary on the Poem	
A Commentary on Part II	
3 The Contexts of *Absalom and Achitophel*	66
The Economic and Social Context	
Political Theory	
Religion	
Whigs and Tories	
Literature and Science	
4 Satire	85
Conventions used in Dryden's *Absalom*	
Dryden's Rejection of Rough Satire	
Satire and the Heroic	
Panegyric	
Dryden's Discourse	
Lampoon	
5 Biblical Allegory and Typology	98
Key to the Allegory	
6 The Heroic Couplet	104
Bibliography	111

Introduction

We all have had the experience of wishing to share our pleasure in a poem, a painting, or a piece of music, only to find our friends unwilling to make an initial effort to understand the conventions and special characteristics of the work. We often forget that we too had resisted the necessary initiation, and only entered the stage of enjoyment and familiarity after the fundamentals had been grasped. We learn to walk before we can run in the world of art as much as in the physical world.

Dryden's *Absalom and Achitophel* is a poem which yields great aesthetic and intellectual pleasure, but only when the reader is given friendly guidance over the unfamiliar ground of seventeenth-century culture and history. The poem is the focus of a rich web of meanings, drawn from the Bible, literary tradition, social, economic and political histories and a major political crisis of the day. It was both deeply traditional and utterly modern. It assumed the reader's lively engagement with both the literature of Greece and Rome, with popular uses of the Bible and with the newly evolving party politics of Charles II's reign. It is possible to recreate much of the delight which was expressed by readers of the time, even though the political nature of the poem meant that it could hardly be enjoyed by the Whigs, whom Dryden attacks. In this respect the passage of time will have broadened the potential readership, for we can hardly feel caught up in the same passionate debates which threatened to tear Restoration society apart. Nevertheless, we can imaginatively enter into Dryden's conservative view of society without feeling threatened about our own convictions. We may even be amused to discover that certain Restoration attitudes and prejudices still shape modern British politics. Whatever our ideological response we are still free to appreciate the remarkable literary skill which Dryden deploys in satirizing his contemporaries.

After a brief biographical survey the second chapter of this book is devoted to a substantial commentary on the first part of the poem and that portion of the second part believed to be Dryden's. The commentary includes elucidation of literary and historical details needed for the immediate comprehension of the poem, as well as some passages of literary analysis to help the reader appreciate Dryden's technical prowess. The remaining chapters should be regarded as appendices to the commentary: they provide a fuller and more extensive historical examination of the

Masterstudies: Absalom and Achitophel

social, political, religious and literary material which is woven into the poem. The commentary uses cross-references to direct the reader to more extensive discussions of issues it touches upon only briefly.

The dedication of this book to Harold Brooks is a small token of my esteem for a friend and mentor, who over the years has done more than he knows to strengthen my understanding of the values and discipline of literary and historical scholarship. This book's strengths but not its weaknesses are owing largely to him.

1 Dryden's Life and Writings

Like T. S. Eliot, who admired him, Dryden favoured an impersonal approach to poetry. Eliot went out of his way to discourage biographers, insisting that his poetry was not an expression of his life, but rather an aesthetic process which allows the poet to *escape* from the confines of personality and mere individuality. Eliot's poetry appeals to readers for reasons that do not relate to his life. He gives us, in his early poetry, an acute sense of cultural breakdown and spiritual crisis. Dryden's poetry has no such modernistic appeal. He was the supreme public poet, and wrote from a position of calm authority and cultivated good sense. Like Eliot he drew on the rich tradition of classical and Christian culture. Dryden was able to work creatively within the conventions and genres established by the classics and developed by his immediate predecessors. He was supremely gifted as a synthesizer of literary models and styles. He resembles Eliot in keeping his eye on the ordinary existence of his own society; his poems are full of images of practical life. Eliot's use of tradition differed insofar as he perceived a profound crisis in Western civilization, which required him to assert the values of European culture in an aggressively learned way. Dryden was much more comfortable and confident in the cultural values he took for granted. Even the poetry of Pope, in the eighteenth century, has more sense of cultural crisis than Dryden's. The fourth book of *The Dunciad*, for example, is more tragic and pessimistic than anything in Dryden. Most modern readers seem to prefer poetry and prose which is full of existential *angst* or Christian despair to writing which confidently asserts its beliefs and sees no need to question literary conventions. For all these reasons the modern reader coming freshly to a poem like *Absalom and Achitophel* needs to be slowly and carefully introduced to Dryden's poetic universe. The immediate frissons of Romantic and modernist poetry are not available in Dryden's poetry. There is no great appeal to areas of private and subjective experience, no engagement with the natural world and no mystical or spiritual sublimity. One might say that in Dryden all is sweetness and light, to use a phrase of Matthew Arnold's describing the classical way of writing.

Dryden's impersonality as a writer is echoed in the biographical record. We know very little about his private life and thoughts. Only about eighty of his letters survive, and they, unlike the consciously studied letters of Swift and Pope, are mostly about business affairs. What others said of him during his lifetime adds little to the picture. He had a reputation of being superior and reserved. His relatively humble background and modest means made it necessary for him to be rather pliable and flexible in his demeanour and attitudes, although those who attack him for changing his religion in 1685 tend to overlook the fact that he did not change it back when the Catholic James II was dethroned in 1688. His important poems on religion give us no insight into his personal motives for abandoning his Anglican faith for Catholicism. Sir Walter Scott summarizes the typical aspersions against Dryden which were often repeated during his career:

That Dryden had been bred a Puritan and republican; that he had written an elegy on Cromwell; that he had been in poverty at the Restoration; that Lady Elizabeth Dryden's character was tarnished by the circumstances attending their nuptials; that Dryden had written the 'Essay on Satire' in which the king was libelled; that he had been beaten by three men in Rose Alley; finally, that he was a Tory, and a tool of arbitrary power.

The religious insult is a dubious inference from the fact that Dryden's family were 'Puritan' and supported Cromwell. Their 'dissent', such as it was, probably took the form of rejection of 'Romish' tendencies within the Church of England. The Cromwell poem was certainly written, but Dryden was not unusual in having praised the *de facto* monarch of the day and then performed the same office for Charles II in 1660. There were certainly rumours about Lady Elizabeth, to the effect that she had 'lax morals' when she married Dryden, or that it was a shot-gun wedding. There is no evidence to support either allegation. One should add that she bore Dryden three sons, none of whom outlived their mother. The Rose Alley affair is shrouded in mystery, but Dryden was certainly wrongly identified as the author of the *Essay on Satire*. Dryden was a proud Tory, but did not support arbitrary power. These contemporary attacks and insinuations add nothing to our understanding of Dryden's personality or private life, but he was, in any case, determined to keep them to himself. He wrote that he had every opportunity to reply to attacks on his reputation as a man, but that instead '[I] have suffer'd in silence; and possess'd my Soul in quiet.'

The facts of his life can be stated quite briefly. The following table gives the essential dates of events in his life and of the important publications which relate to poetry. It omits reference to Dryden's large output of dramatic writings. He wrote more than twenty plays in two periods (1663–80 and 1689–93), and more than one hundred prologues and epilogues (many of which are of importance to literary criticism). He also wrote biographies and several political pamphlets as Historiographer Royal (including *His Majesty's Declaration Defended*, which he uses in *Absalom*; see p. 17).

Principal Dates in Dryden's Life and Career

1631	Born 9 August in Northamptonshire, the first of fourteen children. His family on his father's and mother's side supported the Parliamentary forces during the Civil Wars of the 1640s.
c. 1644–50	Attended Westminster School, London, under the famous Dr Busby.
1650–54	Attended Trinity College, Cambridge, leaving with a B.A. degree in 1654.
1657–8	Employed as a clerk in London under the Commonwealth government.
1660	Wrote *Astraea Redux* on the restoration of Charles II.
1662	Elected to the Royal Society.
1663	Married Lady Elizabeth Howard, daughter of the Earl of Berkshire.
1667	*Annus Mirabilis* (on the great fire of London and the naval war with Holland).
1668	Appointed Poet Laureate, and made an M.A. Cantab.
1670	Appointed Historiographer Royal.
1679	Beaten by thugs in Rose Alley, Covent Garden on the order of someone (unknown, and certainly not Rochester) who suspected that he had written *An Essay on Satire*, which contained attacks on the Earl of Rochester. It was in fact by the Earl of Mulgrave, although Dryden may have had a hand in it.
1680	*Ovid's Epistles*. This translation contains an important preface.
1681	*ABSALOM AND ACHITOPHEL*
1682	*The Medal*, *THE SECOND PART OF ABSALOM AND ACHITOPHEL*, and *Religio Laici* (a statement of Dryden's Anglican faith).
1684	*Mac Flecknoe* (written 1676).
1685	James II ascends the throne. Dryden becomes a Catholic.
1687	*The Hind and the Panther* (a statement of Dryden's Catholic faith).

Masterstudies: Absalom and Achitophel

1688	James II dethroned and succeeded by the Protestant William III. Dryden dismissed from posts as Poet Laureate and Historiographer Royal. Under financial pressure, he starts his second period as a playwright in 1689.
1692	*Satires of Juvenal and Persius* (with the *Discourse Concerning . . . Satire*).
1697	*The Works of Virgil.*
1700	Died 1 May.

2 *Absalom and Achitophel:*
A Commentary on the Poem

This chapter starts with a few general observations about *Absalom and Achitophel*, an account of its immediate political context, and an analysis of the poem's structure. The rest of the chapter is devoted to a detailed commentary which follows the divisions given in the analysis. Line references are given in parentheses, and the text used for quotations from the poem is in the second volume of the California Dryden (see Bibliography). Historical and literary points are elucidated where they are required for the understanding of particular passages. However, larger historical or literary questions are dealt with in later chapters.

Dryden blends four main elements in the poem's construction:

(1) The biblical story of Absalom's and Achitophel's conspiracy against King David (from the second Book of Samuel).

(2) The traditional themes of temptation and fall, especially as portrayed in Milton's *Paradise Lost* and *Paradise Regained*.

(3) The history of the English Civil Wars, which was still fresh in people's memories and frequently used by writers as a source of political lessons.

(4) The Tory view of the people and social types involved in the Exclusion Crisis: Shaftesbury the false politician, Monmouth his dupe, the heroic Charles II and the minor roles of malcontents, London mob and the few loyalists.

These fictional and 'real' strains of narrative are welded together with the help of a number of literary genres: epic, satire, panegyric, elegy, character writing, biblical allegory and oratory, all of which are discussed in later chapters. Dryden's originality lies in this amalgamation of disparate genres, which he achieves without abandoning classical tradition. He cleverly avoids following a recognized literary form which would have required him to observe set rules.

Dryden's thinking about the political conflicts of the day had already been developed in the heroic plays, which reflect conflicts between Catholics and Protestants, Whigs and Tories, king and Parliament. The dedication to Danby (Charles's then chief minister) in *All for Love* (1678) contains an attack on republicanism, which he regarded as the worst sort of tyranny: 'For no Christian Monarchy is so absolute, but 'tis

Masterstudies: Absalom and Achitophel

circumscrib'd with Laws.' He continued his attacks on reformers who wished to limit the royal power in the dedications in *Troilus and Cressida* (1679) and *The Kind Keeper* (1679). Dryden, as one would expect, glorifies the court, but is no less critical of absolute monarchs than he is in *Absalom*. *The Duke of Guise* (1682), written with Nathaniel Lee, is very like *Absalom* in theme.

The Immediate Political Context

The poem was a response to a political crisis. The Whig party, led by the Earl of Shaftesbury, had been trying to exclude from the succession to the throne James, Duke of York, brother to King Charles II, on the grounds that James was a Catholic. Although he was converted in 1669, his Catholicism did not become known until 1673, when he resigned as Lord High Admiral following the Test Act, which excluded Catholics from public office. There was some cause for anxiety about the king too, although he kept his Catholic leanings secret. We now know that he promised Louis XIV, in a secret clause of the Treaty of Dover (1670), that he would announce his conversion to Catholicism at an appropriate time. In fact, he never did so, and formally converted to Rome only on his death-bed in 1685. The Whigs regarded themselves as true Protestant patriots who were determined to prevent the succession of a Catholic monarch in a Protestant country which had successfully resisted the Spanish Armada in 1588 and had survived the Gunpowder Plot in 1605. By 1673 the third war against the Dutch was becoming very unpopular, especially since the statholder, William of Orange, was a Protestant cousin of the king.

Between 1678 and 1680 the alleged Popish Plot released violent anti-Catholic passions. There were about 260,000 Catholics (about 4.7 per cent of the population), rather fewer than Dryden's 'Ten to One' (123) suggests. The first 'information' was given during August and September 1678 by Israel Tonge, an Anglican minister. However, Titus Oates, a half-educated Catholic convert (later renegade), soon emerged as the master 'informer'. He deposed on oath before a London magistrate, Sir Edmund Berry Godfrey, that the Catholics planned to murder Charles and to make England a Catholic country. Godfrey's subsequent murder (his body was found in a ditch near Primrose Hill on 17 October 1678) seemed to confirm the plot and led to serious unrest. Many were put to death on the strength of the evidence of Oates and other perjurers, especially Israel Tonge, William Bedloe and Miles Prance. During the frenzy terrible things were done. For example, a young Catholic, William

Absalom and Achitophel: *A Commentary on the Poem*

Staley, was executed for saying to a friend in a pub that he would kill the king. His family buried him ostentatiously, but the Privy Council had his body exhumed and his head displayed on London Bridge. The discovery of treasonable material in the letters of Edward Coleman (written 1674–77), a former secretary to James, suggests that there was something afoot and Coleman was executed. About thirty-five people were executed during the height of the terror in 1678–79. This is not many, considering the manic state of the nation, driven into a panic by the anti-Catholic rantings of politicians, clergy and pamphleteers. The last major trial convicted the so-called Five Jesuits in June 1679. The acquittal in July of Sir George Wakeman, the queen's physician, was very unpopular but proved a turning-point. From then on Oates's 'revelations' were treated with more and more scepticism. Historians believe that certain Catholic lords may have been involved in conspiracy, but that the plot was, nevertheless, to a great extent a fiction.

Fear of Catholicism provided a focus for revolutionary discontent. Shaftesbury championed Oates and pressed forward with an Exclusion Bill in 1680 which would have made way for the succession of the Duke of Monmouth. However, despite Dryden's accusations in the poem, it should be noted that the Whigs were by no means united in their support of Monmouth, and made sure that the rights to succession of Mary (later queen) were secured. Charles faced the dilemma that if he allowed Parliament to sit, it would pass the bill, but if he prorogued it, he would have no source of funds. Having once prorogued and dissolved Parliament in 1680, only to be faced with an equally exclusionist Parliament in 1681, he secretly accepted a subsidy from Louis XIV. This enabled Charles to dissolve the Oxford Parliament on 28 March, throwing the Whig opposition into disorder. On 8 April he appealed to the nation in *His Majesty's Declaration* explaining his motives for dissolving two Parliaments. A reply in *A Letter from a Person of Quality* rejects the king's arguments and warns the nation of the dangers of absolutism and popery. A Tory reply to these Whig objections, *His Majesty's Declaration Defended* (June 1681) was probably written by Dryden. Shaftesbury's influence was thus shaken and he was sent to the Tower on a charge of high treason (2 July). Dryden's Tory poem, probably written on Charles's request, appeared anonymously in November, about one week before Shaftesbury's trial, but did not prevent his acquittal. Narcissus Lutrell's copy was dated 17 November, the probable date of publication, and he ascribed it to Dryden.

Masterstudies: Absalom and Achitophel

The Poem's Structure

The poem's discourse has three levels, all of which are found in epic poems:
   (1) portraits
   (2) speeches
   (3) narrative-descriptive passages

The three levels are interspersed throughout the poem. If we divide the poem into sections, we begin to see that it was carefully structured:

(A) Lines 1–42   David and the illegitimate Absalom introduced
(B) Lines 43–149   A general account of the troubled situation
   (43–68 The fickle 'Jews')
   (69–84 The 'moderate sort' have little influence)
   (85–149 The 'Jebusites' and the plot)
(C) Lines 150–490   The character of Achitophel and his tempting of Absalom
(D) Lines 491–681   The conspirators
   (491–542 The City interests)
   (543–681 Portraits of Zimri, Shimei, Corah and others)
(E) Lines 682–758   Absalom's disloyalty and his 'Royal' progress
(F) Lines 759–810   The political core of the poem: rejection of political revolution
(G) Lines 811–913   The king's wise counsellors (Barzillai, Zadoc and others)
(H) Lines 914–32   Interlude: brief summary
(I) Lines 933–1031   David's intervention

Surveying these units once more, we can detect an effective sequence:

(A) 'Epic' preliminaries: heroic satire on David
(B) *General* situation
(C) ACT I: the temptation scene (Achitophel = Satan)
(D) *Particular* troublemakers
(E) ACT II: the Fall (Absalom = Adam or pseudo-Christ)
(F) *General* political theory
(G) *Particular* wise counsellors
(H) Interlude
(I) ACT III: 'Epic' conclusion: heroic action by David (David = God)

The poem is suitably framed by the opening narrative-descriptive passage (A) about David and by his closing momentous speech (I), the first

Absalom and Achitophel: *A Commentary on the Poem*

satirical, the second heroic; (C), (E) and (I) provide the main action, clearly paralleling the familiar story of man's Fall and salvation; the generality of (B) and (F) is balanced by the particularity of (D) and (G).

A Commentary on the Poem

David and Absalom (1-42)

The poem opens with a daring directness. Dryden knew that the obvious weakness of Monmouth's position was his illegitimacy, and that one of Charles's vulnerable points was his sexual promiscuity. Instead of temporizing and circling the problem, he faces it immediately. He could rely on the constitutionally minded to react against the idea of a bastard succeeding his natural father. Thomas Craig, in *The Right of Succession* (1603) wrote: 'Neither can any man legitimate his bastards'. The wicked Edmund in Shakespeare's *King Lear* spoke of his situation in terms very like Absalom-Monmouth:

> Why bastard? Wherefore base,
> When my dimensions are as well compact,
> My mind as generous, and my shape as true,
> As honest madam's issue? . . .
> . . . Well then,
> Legitimate Edgar, I must have your land.
> Our father's love is to the bastard Edmund,
> As to th' legitimate.

By referring to the Old Testament custom of polygamy Dryden is able to condone Charles's promiscuity in a light-hearted way. The readers would remember their Bible with private amusement: 'And David took him more concubines and wives out of Jerusalem, after he was come from Hebron: and there were yet sons and daughters born to David.' (II Samuel 5:13) Bishop Burnet actually speculated on the question when pondering the problem of the queen's sterility. He came up with a view rather close to Dryden's humorous one: 'David's Wives (and store of them he had) are termed by the Prophet, *God's Gift to him*: Yea, *Polygamy* was made, in some Cases, a *Duty* by *Moses's* Law.'

Dryden neatly proceeds to throw in some satire on the priesthood ('In pious times, e'r Priest-craft did begin' – as if priests go with impiety!). In this anticlericalism Dryden was at one with the majority of his contemporaries, who suspected all priests, whether they were Puritan preachers or the restored Anglican clergy. Anticlerical satire goes back to the middle ages, and occurs frequently in Dryden's other works.

However, the opening lines of the poem are softened by a delicate irony. That priests insist on monogamy can hardly be used by the reader as ammunition against them (the private thoughts of Burnet would hardly have been common knowledge).

Dryden knew that Charles's human weaknesses could not obscure his symbolic greatness as God's representative and upholder of the law. He stands for 'law and order' (last lines: 'their Lawfull Lord'). There are twenty-six occurrences of 'law' and its derivatives, and six of the rhyme 'laws'/'cause'. Dryden's humour is subtly combined with the elevation of 'Godlike David' who does the Lord's work of procreation:

> Then *Israel*'s Monarch, after Heaven's own heart,
> His vigorous warmth did, variously, impart
> To Wives and Slaves: And, wide as his Command,
> Scatter'd his Maker's Image through the Land. (7–10)

To put it bluntly, Dryden is saying that Charles has had sexual intercourse with all and sundry, and has produced an abundance of illegitimate offspring. In view of Charles's ideological strength, Dryden was able to start the poem by acknowledging what the Court wits often made jokes about – Charles's liking for the ladies. He was called Rowley after a famous stud horse! The notorious Earl of Rochester wrote an obscene poem on Charles, which includes the lines:

> Restless he rolls about from whore to whore,
> A merry monarch, scandalous and poor.

Charles had married the Portuguese Catherine of Braganza in 1662. The marriage brought considerable economic benefits to Charles's government at a time when Parliament was unable to satisfy his financial needs, but Catherine proved barren and produced no heir to the throne. Compare II Samuel 6:23: Michal 'had no child unto the day of her death'. The king's many liaisons proved more fertile. The first of his mistresses at the Restoration was Barbara Palmer, who became Lady Castlemaine in 1661 and bore Charles a daughter, Anne, in that year. Barbara lived in the royal household after Charles's marriage, and continued to bear him children. Two other Catholic duchesses were prominent in his bedchamber over the years of his reign: Louise-Renée de Kéroualle, Duchess of Portsmouth, and Hortense Mancini, Duchess of Mazarin. The duchesses were the favourite targets of the court wits whose obscene lampoons provide a lurid portrait of court immorality in Charles's time. His other mistresses, at various times, included Jane

Absalom and Achitophel: *A Commentary on the Poem*

Lane, the fat Mademoiselle de Montpensier, the Duchess of Châtillon, Winifred Wells, Jane Middleton, Lady Chesterfield and of course Nell Gwyn.

Charles's favourite among his many illegitimate children was James, Duke of Monmouth, born in 1649 as a result of his affair with Lucy Walter whom he met during the royalist exile. Charles refused to declare Monmouth legitimate. In the spring of 1680 a rumour was spread that a mysterious black box containing the marriage certificate of Charles and Lucy had been found. Once the Exclusion Crisis was under way Charles solemnly denied the marriage. Dryden distinguishes Monmouth-Absalom from 'this Numerous Progeny' only in physical terms (see also p. 28): there was none

> So Beautifull, so brave as *Absolon*:
> Whether, inspir'd by some diviner Lust,
> His Father got him with a greater Gust;
> Or that his Conscious destiny made way
> By manly beauty to Imperiall sway. (18–22)

Once again Dryden cleverly balances Charles's all too evident sexual weakness ('inspir'd by ... Lust ... His Father got him') against the godlike nature of the act ('diviner'). We will notice that this witty play with opposed attitudes often goes with Dryden's use of the oxymoron. This figure of speech combines words which normally clash, as in 'diviner Lust'. 'Oxymoron' itself is an oxymoron, meaning 'sharp-dull'. Later we meet 'Godlike Sin' and 'pious Hate'.

The poem's open references to Absalom's illegitimacy are a clever political tactic. In one blow Dryden destroys the first premise of the Exclusionist position – that Monmouth was a worthy successor. Dryden is free to praise his good points without wavering in his commitment to legitimate succession. In praising Absalom's renown in 'Foreign fields' (23), he alludes to Monmouth's military service against the Dutch in 1672 and 1673, and against the French in 1678. 'Warlike Absolon' had also put down the Scottish Covenanters' rebellion at Bothwell Bridge in 1679.

It is interesting to note that Dryden had already used the positive side of the biblical Absalom in praising Monmouth in the dedication of the *Indian Emperor* (1667) and *Tyrannick Love* (1669), addressed 'To the most illustrious and high-born Prince'. He wrote, for example, 'You have all the advantages of mind and body, and an illustrious birth, conspiring to render you an extraordinary person.' However, in our poem Dryden introduces a rather sinister note of violence when he refers to

Masterstudies: Absalom and Achitophel

'Amnon's Murther'. Modern scholars have disagreed about the subject of the allusion, but most have considered the most likely candidate to be Sir John Coventry whose nose was slit by a detachment of Life Guards for sarcasm against the king in a speech in the Commons. As commander of the Guards Monmouth was suspected of having instigated this punishment. On the other hand, Dryden may not have expected the reader to look for a specific parallel (see p. 99).

To sum up this section, Dryden makes use of the biblical parallel to defuse the potentially embarrassing fact of Charles's promiscuity, which was in everyone's mind during the crisis. Charles emerges as both human and divine. Monmouth's physical beauty is echoed in the biblical account of Absalom, but is counterbalanced by his headstrong nature and his evident illegitimacy.

God's Pamper'd People (43–68)

Politicians often remind people that history repeats itself. Those in favour of strong military action against external threats usually remind their citizens of the fateful result of Chamberlain's policy of appeasement against Nazi Germany in the 1930s. Anyone adopting a conservative view of politics in the later seventeenth century was always able to touch an anxious nerve by stirring up fears about civil war. The traumatic events of the 1640s, culminating in the execution of Charles I, could not easily be forgotten. While it is true that Cromwell and other Parliamentary leaders were willing to suppress popular movements of dissent and demands for democratic revolution, it was nevertheless firmly established in Restoration myth that constitutional wrangles led to civil war, which in turn encouraged mob rule and general political chaos. There was already available to writers a rich vocabulary of mockery and denigration of the common people, partly derived from classical literature and partly from native tradition. A rich seam of poetic imagery was based upon fear of the 'mob'. Greek and Latin literature and Christian theology are full of precedents. The Latin *'mobile vulgus'* (the fickle crowd) is the origin of the word 'mob'. The great Puritan poets, Spenser and Milton, were both hostile to the idea of democracy. Archbishop Whitgift in the sixteenth century thought that 'the people ... are commonly bent to novelties and to factions, and most ready to receive that doctrine that seemeth to be contrary to the present state.' As Christopher Hill has put it, 'Conservatives always hated anything like an appeal to opinion outside the ruling class.' Even Puritans and Parliamentarians feared what Pym, in 1642, called 'tumults and insurrections

Absalom and Achitophel: *A Commentary on the Poem*

of the meaner sort of people'. The sectaries (Ranters, Diggers, Levellers and others) were much feared for their ability to stir up discontent among the common people, and especially in the army. In 1681 there still remained a strong memory of these times. Dryden's own poetry is full of anti-popular idiom: 'the ignoble crowd', 'the people's rage', the 'many-headed beast', 'the rabble', 'giddy crowds, changeable as winds', are some examples.

'The Jews' (the English) are described (45 ff.) as 'a Headstrong, Moody, Murmuring race', who, 'debauch'd with ease', and 'too fortunately free', 'Began to dream they wanted [lacked] libertie'. The phrases 'debauch'd with ease' and 'too fortunately free' both have the contradictory wit of the oxymoron (see above). The ease and freedom of Charles's reign paradoxically created discontent rather than gratitude. Far from celebrating their freedom, the English demand more. Dryden then (57–60) rapidly surveys the Civil Wars, Commonwealth and Restoration, emphasizing the people's restlessness and lack of direction (first they banished David, then they proclaimed him king again). They are '*Adam*-wits' (51): like the first Adam they are impatient with their freedom under God's law and wickedly yearn for more. The central metaphor of this section of the poem is subtly used to heighten this dangerous fickleness of the people:

> (Gods they had tri'd of every shape and size
> That God-smiths could produce, or Priests devise:)
> ....
> Their Humour more than Loyalty exprest,
> Now, wondred why, so long, they had obey'd
> An Idoll Monarch which their hands had made:
> Thought they might ruine him they could create;
> Or melt him to that Golden Calf, a State. (49–50, 62–6)

The Jews are 'God-smiths', who like goldsmiths melt down precious metal and form it into whatever shape they please. Dryden cleverly insinuates a reference to the making of false images in the Old Testament. The kings they make are their idols, intended for false worship. Later the 'admiring Croud are dazled' by Absalom, and 'on his goodly person feed their eyes' (686–7), and receive him 'as a Guardian God'. The 'Golden Calf' (line 66) is a reference to the episode in Exodus in which the Israelites, impatient at Moses's delay in returning from the mount (32:1), persuaded Aaron to make a calf from the melted down earrings of the people for them to worship. When challenged by Moses, Aaron lamely declares that he cast the gold in the fire 'and there came out this calf' (32:24).

Masterstudies: Absalom and Achitophel

Before discussing the Popish Plot, Dryden reminds us that not all the Jews are so headstrong. Some appreciate 'the value of a peacefull raign' and 'looking backward with a wise afright', learn the lessons of civil dissension:

> The moderate sort of Men, thus qualifi'd,
> Inclin'd the Ballance to the better side: (75–6)

Once again Dryden uses a favourite rhetorical device of the conservative: he calls those who are content with the existing state of affairs 'moderates' and those who question or rebel 'a fickle rout' (785).

The Popish Plot (85–149)

Compared with his violent contempt for the Dissenters and sectaries Dryden's attitude to the Catholics is mild. Critics often point rather cynically to his conversion to Catholicism at the time of James II's succession in 1685. However, it is fair to say that Dryden's Catholicism was not as militant as James's. In *Absalom* Dryden mocks the Catholic doctrine of transubstantiation and their 'idolatry' (118–22), and does not avert his eyes from Catholic attempts to reconvert England (they 'rak'd, for Converts, even the Court and Stews'). Otherwise, he avoids the virulence of Puritan attacks on 'Popery'. Dryden honestly recognizes the extent of the persecution suffered by Catholics:

> Impoverisht, and depriv'd of all Command,
> Their Taxes doubled as they lost their Land, (94–5)

Dryden's assessment of the truth of Titus Oates's 'revelations' about a Popish Plot is remarkable for its balance and judgement. Modern historians, who possess a much more detailed understanding of the facts than Dryden could have had, do not dissent from his version:

> From hence began that Plot, the Nation's Curse,
> Bad in it self, but represented worse:
> Rais'd in extremes, and in extremes decry'd;
> With Oaths affirm'd, with dying Vows deny'd:
> Not weigh'd, or winnow'd by the Multitude;
> But swallow'd in the Mass, unchew'd and Crude.
> Some Truth there was, but dash'd and brew'd with Lyes ... (108–14)

Dryden correctly understood that the accusations of Oates and others were a gross fabrication. However, the intrigues revealed in the letters of Coleman and the secret clauses of the Treaty of Dover certainly show that there was 'some truth' in the idea of a plot. It is also true that a

Absalom and Achitophel: *A Commentary on the Poem*

great deal of political capital was being made out of it by the Whigs. Typically, Dryden puts the blame on the gullibility of the 'Multitude'. The fourth line of the quotation alludes to the oaths and perjuries of the witnesses who brought men to their deaths, and to the dying vows of the Five Jesuits (Thomas Whitebread, John Gavan, Anthony Turner, John Fenwick and William Harcourt) who denied on the scaffold (20 June 1679) having murdered Godfrey.

Dryden recognized that the potential danger of the plot was not religious but political. His warnings are couched in the conservative imagery of excess:

> For, as when raging Fevers boyl the Blood,
> The standing Lake soon floats into a Flood;
> And every hostile Humour, which before
> Slept quiet in its Channels, bubbles o'r:
> So, several Factions from this first Ferment,
> Work up to Foam, and threat the Government. (136–41)

The central image is of flood, which causes the overflow of channels and spreads destruction all around. The image of a river bursting its banks was Shakespeare's favourite for describing political anarchy. The image also has good classical precedent. Compare Dryden's own version of Virgil's description of Neptune's calming of the storm which Juno sends to obstruct Æneas. Interestingly, the metaphor is the reverse in structure: Neptune is like a noble orator who 'soothes with sober words [the] angry mood' of the 'ignoble crowd' ('mad are their motions, and their tongues are loud'). Dryden's diction is full of emotive words: 'raging', 'hostile', 'bubbles o'r', 'Factions', 'Ferment', 'Foam', 'threat'. Note also the alliteration (*f*actions, *f*erment, *f*oam), often used in the poem to raise the political temperature.

Achitophel's Temptation of Absalom (150–490)

The portrait of Achitophel is carefully designed to contrast with David's and to complement Absalom's. David's fondness for his son shows in his desire to be lenient and to leave open the possibility of reconciliation: 'How easie 'tis for Parents to forgive'. (958; this line was added later to soften still further the satire on Monmouth). Dryden the narrator declares, ' 'Tis Juster to Lament him [Absalom], than Accuse' (486). Dryden wants to present David as an indulgent father who ultimately turns his severity on Achitophel for misleading Absalom.

The historical Shaftesbury fought for the king early in the Civil Wars,

Masterstudies: Absalom and Achitophel

but in 1644 went over to the Parliamentary side, and was prominent in Commonwealth politics from 1652. He resisted approaches from the exiled Charles during the 1650s, but was actively working for the restoration of the king early in 1660. Then followed a series of honours and appointments in Charles's new government. In 1672 he was made an Earl and lord chancellor. But by 1673 he had lost the king's favour and steadily became identified as a powerful Protestant grandee, who argued relentlessly against what he regarded as the growing arbitrariness of the court. He was imprisoned in the Tower in 1677 with other parliamentarians for arguing against the king on a constitutional issue. A violently anti-Catholic speech in 1678 was construed as an attack on the Duke of York. In these ways he contributed to the climate of opinion which was to be so receptive to Oates's allegations.

As we have seen, the Whigs and their supporters are associated with images of restlessness and excess. The portrait of Achitophel is no exception. His qualities are rapidly outlined:

> Sagacious, Bold, and Turbulent of wit:
> Restless, unfixt in Principles and Place;
> In Power unpleas'd, impatient of Disgrace:
> A fiery Soul, which working out its way,
> Fretted the Pigmy Body to decay:
> And o'r inform'd the Tenement of Clay.
> A daring Pilot in extremity;
> Pleas'd with the Danger, when the Waves went high
> He sought the Storms; but for a Calm unfit,
> Would Steer too nigh the Sands, to boast his Wit. (153–62)

The Augustan suspicion of energy ('fiery Soul') and intelligence ('Sagacious') is nowhere more apparent than in these powerful lines. However, Dryden never resorts to crude tactics; he never insults, gratuitously maligns, or loses his temper. Even though he is dealing with a serious threat to the crown, he preserves a tone of common sense and balanced judgement. This is not just a matter of temperament but of satiric tactics. Dryden shows that neo-classical restraint is more effective than violent indignation. His lines on Achitophel are packed with thought. Each one justifies a careful analysis. Consider 'In Power unpleas'd, impatient of Disgrace'. First, we note the antithesis 'Power'/'Disgrace'. A statesman may be either in power or may be disgraced and out of office. Either way, Achitophel is unsatisfied: there is no pleasure in the secure possession of power, and disgrace only makes him impatient to seize power again. He is only 'Pleas'd with the Danger'. As a 'Pilot' he

Absalom and Achitophel: *A Commentary on the Poem*

enjoys only dangerous seas; when the sea is calm he seeks out danger by steering 'too nigh the Sands'. Dryden here draws on the traditional metaphor of the ship of state, which needs a safe pilot to guide it through the storms of disorder, not a reckless steersman. Dryden often returns to this reckless side of Achitophel's nature, finding new metaphors to clinch the point:

> But wilde Ambition loves to slide, not stand;
> And Fortunes Ice prefers to Vertues Land: (198–9)

Daring Achitophel prefers to try his luck and risk a fall in attempting to achieve greatness than to abide by law and order and keep his footing. Note how 'slide' goes with 'Ice', and 'stand' with 'Land', and how rhyme gives the latter pair a *steady* harmony. Lines 173–4, another compressed couplet, summarize his perverse nature:

> In Friendship False, Implacable in Hate:
> Resolv'd to Ruine or to Rule the State.

Whether he is a friend or an enemy, he is equally dangerous, but in opposite ways: as a friend he lacks commitment and cannot be relied upon (a friend is someone you can trust); as an enemy he is totally committed – his hatred never lets up. As a politician his restless energy is expressed in *resolution*, but only to take things to extremes: either to have complete personal control of the political machine, or, if that is not possible, to destroy it entirely. This glances at the fact that Shaftesbury had been a leading figure in Charles's government before he decided to lead the Whigs in opposition.

At the heart of the portrait, lines 156–8, is an inimitable image of his self-destructive energy. The triple rhyme (a triplet) is used to give the lines a clinching finality of judgement. The first line gives us a pure image of energy, which appears to promise a grandeur, appropriate to an epic hero – an Achilles or a Turnus. However, the second and third lines divert the image into a destructive direction: the fiery soul proves too fierce for the mortal flesh to support. The image conveys the conflict between body and soul which motivates Achitophel's career. It is, in a way, still heroic, but rather in the way that Milton's Satan is heroic (in the early books of *Paradise Lost*). However, the possibility of true heroic status is immediately denied in the description of his son,

> ... that unfeather'd, two Leg'd thing, a Son:
> Got, while his Soul did hudled Notions try;
> And born a shapeless Lump, like Anarchy. (170–2)

Masterstudies: Absalom and Achitophel

Dryden contemptuously applies to Shaftesbury's son the definition of man attributed to Plato: 'A two-legged unfeathered animal'. The insult points up the irrationality of Shaftesbury's ambition: he had no heir capable of inheriting the power he sought. But further, he pointedly contrasts this dull conception with Monmouth's at the beginning of the poem: 'inspir'd by some diviner Lust,/His Father got him with a greater Gust'. Monmouth was 'beautiful' and 'brave', not 'a shapeless Lump'. This contrast increases the distance between Absalom and Achitophel, emphasizes the regal aspect of the king's son, and makes it natural to lay the blame upon Achitophel rather than Absalom.

How objective is Dryden's picture of Achitophel? Certainly he acknowledges Shaftesbury's discernment and incorruptibility as lord chancellor (lines 186–91), though some have regarded the lines as ironic. However, aside from the astute moral and psychological characterization, party politics is very prominent. A link between Parliamentary opposition and the unruly mob is continually asserted: 'none can sin against the Peoples Will'; he 'lent the Croud his Arm to shake the Tree'; he 'Held up the Buckler of the Peoples Cause'; he 'fills the ears/ Of listning Crowds, with Jealosies and Fears' (210–11). We are told that the 'giddy Jews' were ready for a change of government every twenty years, and that Achitophel's choice of Absalom as tool of his designs was part of his courting of the people:

> ... he [Achitophel] knew, his [Absalom's] Title not allow'd,
> Would keep him still depending on the Crowd:
> That Kingly power, thus ebbing out, might be
> Drawn to the dregs of a Democracy. (224–27)

The alliterating 'D's add to the damning effect. In hoping that the new king would be less likely to act arbitrarily and without Parliament's consent, Shaftesbury was, in fact, anticipating the approach of 'constitutional monarchy', heralded by the Glorious Revolution of 1688. One should note, however, that Shaftesbury made a disastrous choice of alternative to James's succession. The saner choice was William of Orange, who ultimately became king after James's exile, and proved much less manipulable than Monmouth would have been. The 'limited Command' (299) he offers Absalom is probably to be understood as one involving the sovereignty of Parliament. Dryden shows more hostility to this constitutional aspect of Shaftesbury's plan than to Monmouth's lack of title. Evidently Charles's fondness for his son, his own promiscuity, and the fear of James's Catholicism were reason enough to play down the issue of illegitimacy. However, a reader would have detected the

Absalom and Achitophel: *A Commentary on the Poem*

dishonest evasions of Achitophel, who talks flatteringly to Absalom of his 'Royal Blood' (294), which is correct, but misleadingly so.

Achitophel's first speech (230–302) begins by treating Absalom as the hoped-for saviour of the nation, drawing in numerous biblical parallels and echoes. He then urges him to seize the opportunity before it is gone: 'thy Fruit must be,/Or gather'd Ripe, or rot upon the Tree.' (250–1) The goddess Fortune (or Opportunity) is often depicted in this period seated on a rolling stone. She is bald behind, but her locks stream out before her to be grasped by the opportunist. Dryden puts into Achitophel's mouth a brilliant version:

> Our Fortune rolls, as from a smooth Descent,
> And, from the first Impression, takes the Bent:
> But, if unseiz'd, she glides away like wind;
> And leaves repenting Folly far behind.
> Now, now she meets you, with a glorious prize,
> And spreads her Locks before her as she flies. (256–61)

The second line describes the 'Bent' (compare 'bias' in the game of bowls) which puts the stone into a particular trajectory. After pointing out what happens if opportunity is not seized, Achitophel switches from the general to the particular in a direct appeal to Absalom: 'Now, now she meets you'. Repetition ('Now, now') is used only at moments of special intensity in Augustan verse, which follows classical precedent in this.

Like those of Milton's Satan or Comus, Achitophel's arguments are powerful but spurious. He urges Absalom to compare himself with Charles on the eve of the Restoration, and to grasp the chance to become king. He then pictures Charles as an old man in decline. Achitophel's warnings about the dangers of Charles's flirtations with Louis XIV (281–8) were not without substance, although Dryden would have expected the reader to regard them as intentionally alarmist.

Introducing Absalom's reply Dryden gives us one of his splendid versions of a commonplace idea – that ambition is a lofty emotion but a dangerous one:

> Desire of Power, on Earth a Vitious Weed,
> Yet, sprung from High, is of Cælestial Seed:
> In God 'tis Glory: and when men Aspire,
> 'Tis but a Spark too much of Heavenly Fire. (305–8)

The conflict between the divine and the human is a theme which relates

Masterstudies: Absalom and Achitophel

to Absalom's unfortunate combination of royal and common blood. Charles/David's blood is divine, while Lucy Walter's was mortal. Ambition in a king might be divine, while in a commoner it is 'a Spark too much of Heavenly Fire'. Rather than damn Absalom's ambition as treasonous or downright wicked Dryden presents it as a divine quality which becomes corrupt in the human breast. The phrase 'a Spark too much of Heavenly Fire' once again has the contradictory sense of an oxymoron. The final words of Absalom's reply elaborate this stylistic and thematic pattern, bringing out the terrible instability and vulnerability of his position:

> Yet oh that Fate Propitiously Enclind,
> Had rais'd my Birth, or had debas'd my Mind;
> To my large Soul, not all her Treasure lent,
> And then Betray'd it to a mean Descent.
> I find, I find my mounting Spirits Bold,
> And *David*'s Part disdains my Mothers Mold.
> Why am I Scanted by a Niggard Birth?
> My Soul Disclaims the Kindred of her Earth:
> And made for Empire, Whispers me within;
> Desire of Greatness is a Godlike Sin. (363–72)

The lines are especially significant, because they mark a shift from loyalty and clear-sighted honesty to self-deception and moral wavering. He had begun by talking of his father's 'unquestion'd Right' and by admitting him 'Good, Gracious, Just, observant of the Laws . . . Enclin'd to Mercy'. He also accepts that James is a 'Worthier Head' and his father's 'lawfull Issue'. However, his 'Yet oh' inaugurates a new movement towards temptation. Notice how skilfully Dryden arranges the key terms within the lines: in line 364 'rais'd' balances 'debas'd'; 'large Soul' in line 365 is counterbalanced by 'mean Descent' in line 366. Similarly '*David*'s Part' and 'Mother's Mold', 'Soul' and 'Earth', 'mounting Spirits' and 'Niggard Birth' sustain the effect. The bitter conflict in Absalom is clinched in the final oxymoron 'Godlike Sin'. We remember that Milton's serpent told Eve 'yee shall be as Gods'.

Achitophel's second and most effective speech (376–476) uses all the skills of Greek and Roman oratory, just as the serpent did in his conclusive speech to Eve. First he praises Absalom's 'Prodigious Gifts' which, he urges, were not given for nothing. He contrasts Absalom's 'Manly Force' with David's 'Mildness'. He links this weakness with Charles's dependence on Parliament, alluding to the financial difficulties which the king finally overcame by accepting secret aid from Louis XIV.

Absalom and Achitophel: *A Commentary on the Poem*

He proceeds to play on the nation's fears of a Catholic successor, and predicts that Charles will eventually, from financial need, 'pass' Absalom's 'doubtfull Title into Law'. Notice that here Achitophel openly and brazenly acknowledges the facts. His next statement is daring and treasonous: if David does not yield, 'the People have a Right Supreme/To make their Kings; for Kings are made for them.' Here he adopts a dangerous interpretation of Hobbes's political theory (see p. 72). Dryden cleverly damns the argument by making Achitophel cite the precedent of the regicides' decision to unmake a king in 1649:

> The *Jews* well know their power: e'r *Saul* [Cromwell] they Chose,
> God [Charles I] was their King, and God they durst Depose. (417–18)

The couplet faithfully reflects the biblical story of the Israelites' rejection of God and their choice of Saul as king (I Samuel 8–10), and at the same time neatly comments on the dramatic events of 1649 and the years following.

Achitophel tries to undermine the filial and paternal bond by persuading Absalom not to be moved by his father's 'Kindness' (the word referred partly to the natural bonds of blood; compare 'kin'). He paints a picture of James as a slumbering lion awaiting the moment to destroy his rival. Such a scenario seems to justify the bleak alternatives:

> Resolve on Death, or Conquest by the Sword,
> Which for no less a Stake than Life, you Draw;
> And Self-defence is Natures Eldest Law. (456–8)

Lines 456–476 are a bold and sagacious incitement to rebellion. Hesitation will give the people a chance to have second thoughts. Turn the tables on your enemies by proclaiming that you are taking up arms 'in the King's Defence'! This alludes to the royalist jibe, frequently repeated during the Civil Wars, against the Long Parliament's claim (in the Militia Ordinance and the Defence of the Militia Ordinance) that the Militia was raised to protect the king and in his name. Royalist satirists were fond of mocking the claim:

> 'Tis to defend his Majesty
> That we against him fight
> *Alexander Brome*

The Act of Uniformity (1662) required that priests and teachers should declare their abhorrence of 'the traitorous position that arms may be taken by [the king's] authority against his person'. Achitophel proceeds

Masterstudies: Absalom and Achitophel

to argue that perhaps David's love for his son will 'Controul' his 'fear'. The last lines are a masterpiece of guile:

> If so, by Force he wishes to be gain'd,
> Like womens Leachery, to seem Constrain'd:
> Doubt not, but when he most affects the Frown,
> Commit a pleasing Rape upon the Crown.
> Secure his Person to secure your Cause;
> They who possess the Prince, possess the Laws. (471–6)

The picture of Charles as a coy woman pretending to say no is hilariously incongruous. The wit shows Achitophel's daring mind, but does not disguise the fact that he is proposing a violent seizure of power in order to compel the king to comply with the demand for exclusion. The argument that Monmouth would be doing only what the king really wants is calculated to remove any guilt Monmouth would feel about being disloyal.

At this point, Dryden might well have made an open attack on the Shaftesbury-Monmouth plot, but he prefers to soften the blame attaching to the tempted Absalom: ' 'Tis Juster to Lament him, than Accuse.' (486) This tactic shows Dryden's commitment to Horatian moderation (see pp. 89 and 94).

Despite Dryden's self-control, this section of the poem succeeds in suggesting that Shaftesbury was the most impressive and the most dangerous actor in the ongoing political drama. Some of Dryden's finest verses are devoted to Achitophel, just as Milton's are to Satan and to Comus. Evil is often attractive and persuasive: the perversion of the highest abilities is both fascinating and appalling. We are reminded of Milton's view of Satan in Book I of *Paradise Lost*:

> his form had not yet lost
> All her Original brightness; nor appeard
> Less than Arch-Angel ruind, and th' excess
> Of Glory obscur'd:

The Conspirators (491–681)

Dryden's survey of the 'Malecontents' who united behind Shaftesbury is an acute analysis, but at the same time a very biased one. He draws attention to several motives of the groups he describes: political, economic and religious. As he puts it, Achitophel sees that their 'several Ends' can be made to 'serve the same Design' (494). He also ranks them by degree of hostility to government: firstly, those who are misled by patriotic feelings; secondly, those who are motivated by self-interest; thirdly, anti-monarchists pure and simple; and lastly, and most dangerously, the London mob. Let us take them in order:

495–500: 'The Best', the Whig Parliamentary leaders, whose main aim is to curb monarchical power. They represent the interests of property and insist that it should be sacrosanct, even if that meant restraining the monarch's power (see section on Locke, p. 73).
501–4: the merchants, who take advantage of the crown's financial difficulties and profit by lending it money at high rates of interest.
505–8: the anti-monarchists, who believe that the crown is simply a drain on the economy.
509–10: the demagogues who stir up the mob.
511–42: the most dangerous faction, the '*Solymæan* Rout' (see also p. 78) – the London rabble who are the dupes of religious fanatics of all kinds: first, the Presbyterian ministers ('*Levites*'), who had fought for control of the kingdom during the Civil Wars and favoured a strict Church government, but who had been forced to leave the Church of England in 1662 by the Act of Uniformity; then the sectaries (see p. 76); and finally the general rabble, 'Who think too little, and who talk too much'. (534)

Notice how the Presbyterians and sectaries are treated as part of the 'Rout', and then as separate groups. The last section concludes with a reference to the much-dreaded masses:

> Such were the tools; but a whole Hydra more
> Remains, of sprouting heads too long, to score. (541–2)

Among the many precedents for this insulting view of the common people are the words (*c.* 1600) of Thomas Dekker referring to 'that wild beast multitude . . . this many-headed Cerberus,/ This pied chameleon, this beast multitude'. It is always easy to treat one's enemies as part of a single conspiracy rather than to recognize their often different motivations. Dryden skilfully blends this kind of conspiracy theory with a more honest intellectual analysis. Nevertheless, his account is biased in its treatment of individual tendencies. On the sectaries, he declares:

> A numerous Host of dreaming Saints succeed;
> Of the true old Enthusiastick breed:
> 'Gainst Form and Order they their Power employ;
> Nothing to Build and all things to Destroy. (529–32)

Everything is studiedly damning: 'dreaming Saints' and 'Enthusiastick breed' pander to all the old cavalier prejudices (see p. 79). Their dreaminess is no indication of quiescence; quite the contrary: they think only in terms of destroying the established order. Cromwell himself had found the Saints (as some of the old Parliamentarians called themselves) a nuisance, and when turning out the Barebones Parliament declared 'There is nothing in the hearts of these men but "Overturn" '. Later (see p. 42) Dryden, in more serious vein, gives us a justification of his view of government. The last lines of his survey hit at the Calvinist strain in dissenting religion:

> Born to be sav'd, even in their own despight;
> Because they could not help believing right. (539–40)

The faithful are 'predestined' to be saved according to Calvinist theology; they receive grace quite apart from their own deserving. It was easy for a sceptical mind like Dryden's to mock such religious ideas. Even a Puritan like Milton had difficulty in swallowing them. Dryden's political point is clear: people who believe that 'they could not help believing right' cannot be relied on to observe laws which do not accord with their beliefs. Such people make good revolutionaries, as they had in the 1640s.

ZIMRI

Having surveyed the general profile of the enemy, Dryden turns to particular cases. He was very proud of his portrait of Zimri, lines 544–68 (see p. 95). There are two biblical Zimris: one is a brazen fornicator (Numbers 25:6–14), the other a conspirator (I Kings 16:9–20). George Villiers, second Duke of Buckingham, had been the king's chief minister after the fall of Clarendon in 1667, but he had turned against the king during the troubled period before the Popish Plot. He had been a boyhood companion of the king's during the exile in France. The bad influence he had on the king, according to Bishop Burnet, is not mentioned by Dryden for obvious tactical reasons, except through the possible reference to the first biblical Zimri. Burnet wrote:

He was bred with the King: And for many years he had a great ascent over him ... he laid before him his schemes, both with relation to religion and politics, which made deep and lasting impressions on the King's mind. So that the main blame of the King's ill principles, and bad morals, was owing to the Duke of Buckingham.

Dryden's conception of Zimri required that this corrupt side of Buckingham's nature should be ignored, or at least treated lightly. The portrait contrasts brilliantly with Achitophel's. While the satanic Shaftesbury is treated as a clever villain, Buckingham is depicted as an incompetent fool. Bernard Schilling contrasts the two characters well:

Absalom and Achitophel: *A Commentary on the Poem*

... it takes a certain amount of talent to be wicked, like Achitophel or his superior, Satan; it demands character of a sort that might do good in the world if properly used. Zimri simply does not show the qualities of a gifted scoundrel; he cannot lead any enterprise, even one that is wrong; he is merely futile.

The germ of characterization is partly taken from Horace's Tigellius (in *Satires* I.2 and I.3) and Juvenal's Greekling (in *Satire* III). These characters, like Zimri, are *inconsistent* and jacks-of-all-trades. Here is Dryden's own translation of Juvenal's description of the Greekling:

> Who bears a nation in a single man?
> A cook, a conjuror, a rhetorician,
> A painter, pedant, a geometrician,
> A Dancer on the ropes, and a physician.

John Oldham's imitation of this passage, which modernizes the Greek to a Frenchman, was written about a year after *Absalom*, but fifteen years before Dryden's translation:

> A needy monsieur can be what he please,
> Groom, page, valet, quack, operator, fencer,
> Perfumer, pimp, Jack-pudding, juggler, dancer.

Dryden's picture of Zimri clearly draws generally on this conception, but excels it in wit and elegance:

> A man so various, that he seem'd to be
> Not one, but all Mankinds Epitome.
> ....
> But, in the course of one revolving Moon,
> Was Chymist, Fidler, States-Man, and Buffoon:
> Then all for Women, Painting, Rhiming, Drinking; (545–6, 549–51)

Zimri is less fully individualized than Achitophel. He is cast more in the mould of a 'Theophrastan character' (Theophrastus was the Greek originator of the formal character sketches of recognizable human and social types). He is 'the inconstant man'. Of course, all characterization of individuals must inevitably draw upon such commonplaces. The skill is to apply them freshly and make them seem individual. David Nicol Smith once pointed out that Samuel Butler's 'character' of our Duke blends the 'Theophrastan character' and the 'historical character': 'The satire on a man of pronounced individuality is heightened by describing his eccentricities as if they belonged to a recognized class.' The biblical name of Zimri added connotations of intrigue and restlessness.

Dryden underlines Zimri's extremism with the ironic phrase 'to shew

Masterstudies: Absalom and Achitophel

his Judgment' (556), which makes the essential neo-classical and humanist point that Zimri *lacks* judgement and good sense. How could a man who cannot govern himself govern others? Dryden then summarizes the dismal career of Buckingham. Dryden's astuteness is apparent in all the details. For example, Zimri 'sought Relief' from his failures at court 'By forming Parties, but coud ne're be Chief'. In David Ogg's account of the various opposition groups which sprang up in 1674 during the third Dutch War he mentions Buckingham's attempt 'to create a following' from 'Presbyterians and old Commonwealth men', 'but without much success'. The general instability of Zimri is evoked by association with the 'revolving Moon', and we remember that the 'giddy Jews' were also 'govern'd by the *Moon*', as are all lovers and madmen.

In the interlude between Zimri's portrait and Shimei's Dryden passes over disdainfully the minor actors in the intrigue. He adds:

> Nor shall the Rascall Rabble here have Place,
> Whom Kings no Titles gave, and God no Grace: (579–80)

We have already discussed Dryden's contempt for the common people (see p. 22 for its political significance). Alliteration often comes to his aid when he wishes to damn them: 'Turn Rebell, and run Popularly Mad' (335); 'Popularly prosecute the Plot' (490); 'My Rebel ever proves my Peoples Saint' (976). The dissenters in religion (and perhaps most of us) would have objected strongly to Dryden's suggestion that lack of 'Titles' goes with lack of God's 'Grace'.

SHIMEI

Dryden returns to his attack on the City of London and dissenting tradesmen in his portrait of Shimei, who, in II Samuel 16, leads the people, and curses and casts stones at David. This alludes to Slingsby Bethel, advocate of religious toleration and free trade, who was elected one of London's two sheriffs in 1680 (see 593–4). His election was managed by the Whigs in order to pack the juries with men of their party (see 607). The acquittal of Shaftesbury a week after the publication of Dryden's poem depended on such political manoeuvering. His 'Zeal to God, and Hatred to his King' (586) neatly picks up the line 'Whom Kings no Titles gave, and God no Grace', discussed above. The reader supplies the corollary: Shimei will receive no title from the king, and his 'Zeal' will draw down no grace from God. The combination of religious 'Zeal' and political 'hate' is used by Dryden to create an incongruous and witty effect, culminating in the oxymoron 'pious Hate'. Another figure used to good advantage is the 'paraprosdokian' (the 'against-expectation'), which leads the reader's thoughts along one path, and then unexpectedly changes direction:

> Did wisely from *Expensive* Sins refrain,
> And never broke the Sabbath, *but for Gain*:
> Nor ever was he known an Oath to vent,
> Or Curse *unless against the Government*.
> Thus, heaping Wealth, by the most ready way
> Among the Jews, *which was to Cheat and Pray*; (587–92; my italics)

The italicized phrases are 'unexpected'. Without them Shimei's behaviour would seem pious in Puritan terms, properly rejecting sin, blasphemy and sabbath-breaking, and pursuing the efficient conduct of one's profession. Dryden makes full use of traditional anti-Puritan satire (see p. 78), emphasizing Shimei's hypocrisy, zeal and stinginess (Bethel's neglect of hospitality when sheriff was notorious). As usual Dryden finds extremism hidden beneath the surface of Puritan righteousness: 'Cool was his Kitchen, tho his Brains were hot.' (621) His attack on Shimei's hypocrisy is so subtle that some critics have misunderstood it. The following lines evidently suggest an ironic parallel between Shimei and Christ:

> [He] lov'd his wicked Neighbour as himself:
> When two or three were gather'd to declaim
> Against the Monarch of *Jerusalem*,
> *Shimei* was always in the midst of them: (600–3)

The second line refers to Christ's promise: 'For where two or three are gathered together in my name, there am I in the midst of them' (Matthew 18:20). The rather blasphemous comparison is ironical in the sense that it is the sort of self-righteous attitude which a Puritan would adopt. Shimei's pretended Christian fellow-feeling is in contrast to a true Christ-like love.

Shimei combines several of the qualities attacked in earlier passages of general analysis. He has the 'Zeal' of the Levites (Nonconformist ministers), and their 'godly Cause'. He too sees no economic value in the monarchy ('Kings were Useless, and a Clog to Trade'). This view was reflected in his anonymously published *Interests of Princes and States* (1680).

CORAH

Dryden's final portrait in this section is of Corah (a rebel against Moses and Aaron in Numbers 16), who is Titus Oates, the fabricator of the Popish Plot. It opens, unusually, with a direct address to Corah:

Masterstudies: Absalom and Achitophel

> Yet, *Corah*, thou shalt from Oblivion pass;
> Erect thy self thou Monumental Brass:
> High as the Serpent of thy metall made,
> While Nations stand secure beneath thy shade. (632–5)

Formally this is pure mock-heroic: a vulgar subject is incongruously treated in heroic style. Dryden combines biblical and classical sources. First, he compares Corah with the brazen serpent made by Moses which protected the children of Israel from a plague of fiery serpents (Numbers 21:9). 'Brass' also had connotations (and still does) of impudence ('as bold as brass'). Dryden also echoes the classical poets who traditionally hope that their verses will provide them with a permanent memorial. Horace, for example, wrote (*Odes* III.30): *'Exegi monumentum aere perennius'* ('I have erected a monument more lasting than bronze'). Of course, Dryden is saying that Oates's notoriety as a liar and false witness will live for ever!

Son of a Norfolk weaver, Titus Oates left Cambridge without a degree, became an Anabaptist preacher, but was ejected from his living in 1673. He became a Catholic in 1677, was expelled from Jesuit colleges in Europe and returned to London in 1678. He invented the plot with the help of a fanatical anti-Jesuit, Israel Tonge. Dryden draws attention to Oates's humble origins ('Weavers issue'), and neatly links this with his earlier contempt for the untitled rabble when he ironically declares that Oates's great work for the 'Publick Good .. Enobles all his Bloud' (640–1). In fact, Oates, once in possession of a pension from Parliament, was embarrassed by his birth and tried to discover himself an ancient pedigree and to live like a gentleman. He claimed to have been made a Doctor of Divinity by the University of Salamanca but the authorities there denied it (see lines 658–9).

As a perjurer Oates had no equal. Dryden's summary is apt:

> His Memory, miraculously great,
> Could Plots, exceeding mans belief, repeat;
> Which, therefore cannot be accounted Lies,
> For humane Wit could never such devise. (650–3)

Although his first efforts to convince Charles and his minister Danby were not successful, he sustained his lies and inventions with an amazing consistency. Having forged Jesuit letters to James's confessor, Bedingfield, he later convinced a Parliamentary committee that they were authentic! After the murder of Godfrey (see p. 16), when the nation was at its most credulous, he produced the names of the provisional government which the 'plotters' proposed to bring in, but began to overreach himself when he accused the queen of complicity with her physician, Wakeman, in a plan to poison Charles. Dryden is not completely ironic when he says

> His Judgment yet his Memory did excel;
> Which peic'd his wondrous Evidence so well:
> And suited to the temper of the times; (660-3)

Dryden once more colours the portrait with the Augustan poet's favourite anti-Puritan terms: 'Saintlike', 'Prophet', 'Visionary', 'Zeal' (twice). He casts him incongruously in the role of the neo-Platonic mystic:

> Some things like Visionary flights appear;
> The Spirit caught him up, the Lord knows where: (656-7)

Such lofty thoughts, absurd and pretentious to the neo-classical mind, are shown to be hypocritical when taken with Oates's brutal hounding of the innocent. The reference to Corah's calling for '*Agag*'s murther' (676) was once thought to refer to the murder of Godfrey, but is more likely to represent Lord Stafford, who was condemned to death in December 1680 on Oates's evidence. The identification is made more likely by the link between the manner of Agag's death ('Samuel hewed Agag in pieces' – I Samuel 15:33) and Stafford's sentence of hanging, drawing and quartering. Charles's remission of the sentence was resented by the Whigs.

The portraits in this section of the poem resemble a rogues' gallery or the chamber of horrors in Madame Tussaud's: there is distortion and bias, but there is also power and vitality in the portraiture. We must also remember that they are actors in a contemporary political crisis which seemed about to turn back the clock to the 1640s. Dryden's readers would have relished the wicked accuracy of Dryden's pen and the majestic way in which he damns his enemies.

Absalom's Pseudo-Royal Progress (682-758)

Having prepared the ground so carefully with anti-popular rhetoric, Dryden now boldly makes Absalom's fall from grace consist of a grovelling attempt to court popularity with 'Th' admiring Croud' who are dazzled by his 'goodly person'. He now takes on the role of tempter – of the people. Just as the biblical Absalom 'stole the hearts of the men of Israel' (I I Samuel 15:6), so Dryden's Absalom 'glides unfelt into their secret hearts' (693). The serpent's guile is also evoked in the word 'glide'. He uses all the alluring arts of 'looks ... gestures, and ... words'. The powerful spell he casts is well expressed:

> Then with a kind compassionating look,
> And sighs, bespeaking pity ere he spoak,
> Few words he said; (694–6)

The long first clause running over the line is cleverly contrasted with the short opening of the third line. Words are only one part of the dazzling effect.

Absalom's speech takes us into the midst of the political situation in England during 1679 and 1680. Monmouth had been sent into exile in September 1679, but returned without permission in November. He was received by the City with tumultuous acclamation. Charles immediately deprived him of all his civil and military offices, and ordered him out of the country, which order he refused. Monmouth maintained his popularity as the great Protestant hero by publicly worshipping in St Martins-in-the-Fields.

The opening lines of his speech (698 ff.) use ammunition from the oldest sources of Whig tradition. He appeals to a myth which had sustained the passions of the Civil Wars and which continued to inspire republicans and Parliamentarians. It had been propagated with skill by the Parliamentarian and upholder of the common law, Sir Edward Coke. Here is J. P. Kenyon's summary of the theory of the 'Norman Yoke', seen from the point of view of John Lilburne, the Leveller, in 1647:

Coke lent his enormous authority to what was later to be regarded as the Whig view of history: that absolute kingship was a Norman device unconstitutionally imposed [by William the Conqueror and his successors] on the free and equal society of Anglo-Saxon England; but the principles of that society had been reaffirmed in Magna Carta, had never been lost sight of, and were now under the guardianship of Parliament.

Absalom's 'I mourn ... your lost Estate' would have stirred the hearts of the upholders of the 'Good old Cause' (82). Talk of 'Liberties' and 'Arbitrary laws' are part of the same rhetoric. He offers himself as a supporter of 'your dear cause' (700). Dryden clearly wishes to reinforce the idea, already attributed to Achitophel, that Monmouth's rebellion aimed not to strengthen monarchy but to weaken it.

He also takes up the popular anti-Catholic feeling. The poet Andrew Marvell, MP for Hull, had anonymously published a book called *An Account of the Growth of Popery and Arbitrary Government in England*

Absalom and Achitophel: *A Commentary on the Poem*

(1677), which summed up the fear that the restoration of the Catholic religion in this country would involve the imposition of absolute monarchy and the total undermining of Parliament. In June 1680 Shaftesbury had led a new and daring campaign against James and the Court. Absalom refers to two of its themes:

> ... *Jebusites* [Catholics] your Sacred Rites invade.
> My father, whom with reverence yet I name,
> Charm'd into Ease, is careless of his Fame:
> And, brib'd with petty summs of Forreign Gold,
> Is grown in *Bathsheba*'s Embraces old: (706–10)

First, he refers to Louis XIV's subsidies, and secondly to one of Charles's mistresses, whom he chooses for her French origins and Catholic sympathies. Bathsheba (the first syllable is stressed) is Louise-Renée de Kéroualle, who became Duchess of Portsmouth in 1673. Notice also the ambiguous use of 'yet' in the second line: the phrase can mean either 'My reverence is as strong as ever', or 'My reverence has not yet been undermined'.

Like a true demagogue Absalom presents his own motives in the most innocent light. He will sacrifice himself for the sake of the cause. He uses the language of a pious suppliant to suggest his passionate sincerity:

> Take then my tears (with that he wip'd his Eyes)
> 'Tis all the Aid my present power supplies:
> No Court Informer can these Arms accuse,
> These Arms may Sons against their Fathers use, (717–20)

Dryden treats this with heavy irony as is shown by the mock-pathos of '(with that he wip'd his Eyes)'. Absalom's sincerity is further undercut by the sinister play on the word 'Arms'. His 'tears' are metaphorical weapons, properly used by sons to move fathers. However, literal weapons are never far from the surface of the lines, especially in the phrase 'my present power'. We are reminded that Achitophel had urged him to 'Resolve on Death, or Conquest by the Sword' (456).

The next paragraph (723–58) narrates Monmouth's western Progress. He made a series of such pseudo-royal tours in the autumn of 1680, first in Oxford and then in the western counties. His progress was greeted with public demonstrations of support and much shouting of 'No popery, no popery!' In the poem he urges the Whig themes of 'Religion, and Redress of Grievances' (747). He even starts a rumour about the queen (750; see p. 39). We need comment no further on the continued denigration of the 'people' (727–8, 739, 743), who treat Absalom as their 'Messiah'.

Masterstudies: Absalom and Achitophel

Dryden uses the language of panegyric (see p. 91) ironically to describe the success of the progress: 'Fame runs before him, as the morning Star' (733). The paragraph concludes with some transitional lines (753–58) preparing the way for Dryden's central doctrinal statement. The message is clear: do not trust the people.

Political Doctrine (759–810)

The political ideas which motivate the poem have already been clearly implied in Dryden's use of certain key terms – 'people', 'liberty', 'property', 'law', 'public good', 'patriot', 'commonwealth', 'limited command'. We have had reason to comment on the bias built into them. However, Dryden now chooses to present a reasoned defence of his political thought. His arguments are clear and expressed with 'moderation':

(1) He admits the dangers of absolutism (759–64).

(2) The new Whig idea of the state as a social contract is acceptable only if it is understood that the contract is not open for renegotiation (765–76).

(3) He warns of the dangers of popular power (777–94).

(4) He favours preserving the *status quo* with the minimum of tampering.

He presents the reader with a dilemma. Kings cannot be allowed to destroy the laws which protect the citizen. However, if we allow that the 'crowd' can take over the laws, the original contract ('cov'nant') should have clearly permitted such a 'resuming'. Dryden affirms the binding nature of the original contract and compares it with Adam's fall which is binding upon all of us, even though we did not 'consent' to it. Further, there can be no security of private property if sovereignty can be dissolved by force. So, while he acknowledges a dilemma, he makes it clear that he would rather trust a monarch not to be 'Arbitrary' than allow the people to judge the situation, for 'What Standard is there in a fickle rout'? (785) Once again, Dryden astutely associates Parliament with the 'rout': 'Sanhedrins may be/Infected with this Publick Lunacy' (787–8). He echoes Hobbes's arguments (see p. 72) by predicting that the breaking of the contract will result in the end of all government and a return to the dreaded 'state of nature', but Hobbes's contract was one among the people themselves to set up a sovereign and not between the people and the king. It was John Locke, the great Whig political philosopher, who argued that the contract was between sovereign and people. Neither view appealed to Dryden who preferred to accept the authority of a strong sovereign provided that his powers were not abused. Dryden pres-

Absalom and Achitophel: *A Commentary on the Poem*

ents the clearest statement of his argument for royal sovereignty in *The Medal* (see p. 51), in which he praises those who restored the monarchy in 1660:

> Who, to destroy the seeds of civil war,
> Inherent right in monarchs did declare;
> And, that a lawful pow'r might never cease,
> Secur'd succession to secure our peace.
> Thus property and sovereign sway, at last,
> In equal balances were justly cast:

Notice that 'inherent right' has replaced the older idea of 'divine right', and that the notion of a balance between the 'sovereign sway' and 'property' clearly rejects absolutism. The distance between the political groups was really not so very great. However, in the heat of debate the rhetoric was less measured. Dryden's position rests on a rejection of all extremes:

> Our temperate isle will no extremes sustain
> Of pop'lar sway or arbitrary reign,
> *The Medal*

Dryden's own conservative conclusion is contained in the line 'But Innovation is the Blow of Fate' (800). Bernard Schilling calls his chapter on this part of the poem 'The Essay on Innovation'. He argues that Dryden here relies most heavily on the 'Conservative Myth' that society's security and health lies in 'order' and obedience. The use of an architectural metaphor is effective:

> If ancient Fabricks nod, and threat to fall,
> To Patch the Flaws, and Buttress up the Wall,
> Thus far 'tis Duty; but here fix the Mark:
> For all beyond it is to touch our Ark.
> To change Foundations, cast the Frame anew,
> Is work for Rebels who base Ends pursue: (801–6)

Metaphors are powerful things. Dryden could rely on all kinds of traditional associations: God was the first architect who designed all in perfect harmony and symmetry only to be disturbed by the interfering hand of man; a good building has a solid foundation which will resist the depredations of time and accident; discussions of government often rely on the metaphor of edifices, fabric and foundations. Marvell had used the image to support more democratic views in his 'The First Anniversary'. The metaphor is used earlier in the poem, when we are told that Achitophel 'The Pillars of the publick Safety shook' (176), and that the sectaries are determined 'Nothing to Build and all things to Destroy'.

Masterstudies: **Absalom and Achitophel**

(532) Finally, the king is regarded as the central pillar of the state at the end of the poem:

> Kings are the publick Pillars of the State,
> Born to sustain and prop the Nations weight: (953–4)

Just as the narrator compares political innovation with sacrilegious 'touching' of the Old Testament ark (804), so Charles proceeds to remind us of Samson's overthrow of the temple on himself:

> If my Young *Samson* [Absalom] will pretend a Call
> To shake the Column, let him share the Fall: (955–6)

So, to 'change Foundations' is 'work for Rebels who base Ends pursue'. One might object that this is hardly a rational argument. However, the associations here operate at the level of 'myth' or 'ideology', rather than reason. The statement that the traditional monarchy was good is not subject to rational discussion. On this issue Dryden was not prepared to enter into theoretical debate: the significance of the monarchy was a matter of faith. The same is true of his use of the medical metaphor which suggests that rebels are like hypochondriacs who imagine they are ill and make themselves worse by administering unnecessary medicines:

> The Tampering World is subject to this Curse,
> To Physick their Disease into a worse. (809–10)

Their folly is to imagine they are sick (see 756). One may conclude that some of the most potent ideologies work through metaphors rich in associations. Dryden's ideology of monarchy is no exception.

The Wise Counsellors (811–913)

If we look again at our division of the poem's narrative sequence (p. 18) we can see that the doctrinal passage we have just examined is central in more than one sense. It is not simply at the heart of Dryden's thinking but also of the poem's structure. Before it, we were presented with a story of temptation and fall – a story of '*Adam*-wits', who like Adam and Eve look for something new and plunge into sin. After it, in the present section and the next, the pendulum swings back towards virtue and salvation. The 'moderate sort of Men' and their king now definitely incline 'the Ballance to the better side' (76). Charles has few friends (813),

> Yet some there were, ev'n in the worst of days;
> Some let me name, and Naming is to praise. (815–16)

One advantage of there being only few men of worth is that there is no

Absalom and Achitophel: *A Commentary on the Poem*

danger of their being merged into some amorphous group of (God forbid!) the multitude.

BARZILLAI AND HIS SON

Dryden signals to the trained reader that he will use the traditional forms of panegyric and elegy to praise the loyal few and to lament Barzillai's loss of a noble son. First, we are told that 'Naming is to praise' (816), and then Ossory will be 'By me . . . always Mourn'd' (832). The subjects of praise and mourning are heroic individuals in the old Renaissance mould. James Butler, Duke of Ormonde (Barzillai), is 'crown'd with Honour and with Years' (818), like his counterpart in II Samuel, 19:32 who is 'a very aged man, even fourscore years old' (nine years older than Ormonde) and 'a very great man'. Dryden takes the opportunity to rehearse once more the earlier troubles of the monarch. The struggle against 'rising Rebells' in 'Regions Waste, beyond the *Jordans* Flood' (819–20) alludes to Ormonde's attempt to restore Ireland (Jordan's flood is the Irish Sea) to royal control in 1650. He failed in this and was forced to join Charles in Paris ('In Exile', 823). With Hyde (Clarendon) he exerted his influence on Charles during the exile, and also made sure that the Catholic influence was kept to a minimum. A great conciliator, he went along with the offers of toleration expressed in the Declaration of Breda. After the Restoration he 'Return'd' (824) to the king's service. He conforms to the Renaissance ideal of greatness by combining military skill and humane culture.

Ormonde's son, Thomas, Earl of Ossory, distinguished himself in the wars against the Dutch and the French, and died of a fever in 1680. Dryden uses the traditional topics of elegy to create this portrait of a cavalier who died young but with honour. Dryden's elegy to John Oldham who died young in 1683 has similar touches: like Ossory, Oldham set out for a 'Goal' and won his 'Race', though young. Both elegies also have a Virgilian pathos built into the language. Ossory is 'snatcht . . ./By unequal Fates' (Virgil's *'fata iniqua'* from the *Æneid*). Both elegies make use of Virgil's moving lines on the warrior Marcellus, who was to succeed the emperor Augustus, and also died young. The following lines, in Dryden's translation, describes Marcellus's destined greatness:

> Mirror of ancient faith in early youth!
> Undaunted worth, inviolable truth!
> No foe, unpunish'd, in the fighting field
> Shall dare thee . . .

Masterstudies: Absalom and Achitophel

Dryden's earlier lines on Ossory delicately turn the Virgilian allusion to a new purpose:

> Oh Ancient Honour, Oh Unconquer'd Hand,
> Whom Foes unpunish'd never coud withstand! (844–5)

Oldham is actually called 'the young Marcellus of our tongue' and like his Roman original is encompassed by 'fate and gloomy night'. Ossory's military greatness requires a more heroic and elevated treatment than was appropriate for the poet Oldham. Dryden as usual is a master of stylistic 'decorum' (choosing the right words for the right occasion). Schilling summarizes the devices of funeral elegy used by Dryden: 'Emotional exclamations, heightened pathos for the death of a young man [Ossory was actually forty-six!], sententiae, the flight of the soul to Heaven' and image of the perfect life. Dryden uses 'sententiae' (pithy and memorable sayings) throughout the poem, to lend it weight and authority. The Roman poet Seneca was the major classical influence on the fashion for 'sentences', especially in Elizabethan and Jacobean drama. Here are some of Dryden's:

> Short is the date of all Immoderate Fame. (847)

> Plots, true or false, are necessary things,
> To raise up Common-wealths, and ruin Kings. (83–4)

> Great Wits are sure to Madness near ally'd; (163)

> But Innovation is the Blow of Fate. (800)

The elegy concludes with some rather fanciful reflections which are typical of the elegies of Donne and Oldham. The poet not only believes he should have joined the soul of the lamented hero but that perhaps he already has done so:

> Or fled she with his life, and left this Verse
> To hang on her departed Patron's Herse? (858–9)

The poet's soul having returned to earth finds none equal to Ossory.

BISHOPS, JUDGES AND LORDS

The last part of this section surveys more rapidly the other supporters of the king. They belong to the three loyal organs of the state: the Church of England, the judiciary ('Pillars of the Laws'), and the House of Lords ('Loyal Peers'). Having attacked the Catholics and Puritans, Dryden now turns to the loyal Anglicans, who are presumably exempted from Dryden's earlier scornful anti-clericalism ('Priests of all Religions are the same', line 99). Indeed, it is interesting to note that he does not refer to their *religious* qualities at all, but only to their *human* qualities and gifts – of humility (865), hospitality (867), good birth (867), eloquence (869), 'Learning and ... Loyalty' (871). Churches are not mentioned, only colleges. By now, Oxford and Cambridge were firmly controlled by the state church (during and before the Civil Wars, Cambridge, especially Emmanuel College, had been a breeding ground for Puritans). Having mentioned the Archbishop of Canterbury (Zadoc), the Bishop of London (the Sagan), and the Dean of Westminster ('Him of the Western dome'), Dryden alludes to the judges (874–5), and then devotes the rest of the section (876–913) to the 'Loyal Peers'.

TRUE NOBLES

It was natural for Dryden to conclude the study of the loyal few with a group of peers, since, as we have seen, nobility, both outer and inner, is not to be found in the king's enemies (the 'Rascall Rabble ... Whom Kings no Titles gave'). Those among the opposition who are noble in birth or title lack inner nobility; they are 'meer Nobles' (572). True nobility was a central theme of Juvenal's satires. In *Satire* IX he declares: 'You owe me, first, the virtues of the mind; prove yourself pure, one who holds fast to what is good both in word and deed, and I acknowledge you a lord.'

Adriel is John Sheffield, Earl of Mulgrave, author of *An Essay upon Satire* (and therefore 'Sharp judging', line 877). As one of Dryden's patrons he was naturally to be thought of as 'the Muses friend'. He has the qualities of a true Augustan: 'True to his Prince; but not a Slave of State' (879). This ideal was upheld by the great Roman Augustans, Horace and Virgil, who, despite their intimacy with the emperor, upheld the virtue of independence.

Jotham (882) is George Savile, Marquis of Halifax, the famous 'trimmer', who tried to mediate between the Whigs and the Tories. Dryden acknowledges this side of Halifax by saying that he tried 'The worse awhile', but 'then chose the better side' (885). He was a supporter of Shaftesbury from 1674–9. However, his support of the king during the Exclusion Crisis proved conclusive. 'So much the weight of one brave man can doe.' (887) His eloquent speeches in the Lords, 15 November 1680, turned the House against Shaftesbury. Hushai (888), David's friend, who was the chief agent in rejecting the biblical Achitophel's counsel (II Samuel 15–17), is Laurence Hyde, who was First Lord of the Treasury during the Exclusion Crisis. He clearly balances the evil counsel of Achitophel, who, we remember, told Absalom:

Masterstudies: Absalom and Achitophel

> The Thrifty Sanhedrin shall keep him poor:
> And every Sheckle which he can receive,
> Shall cost a Limb of his Prerogative. (390–92)

The selfish 'Thrift' of Parliament, which tries to withhold funds from the king, is contrasted with Hyde's 'frugal care' as Treasurer. Last comes Amiel, who is Edward Seymour, former Speaker of the House of Commons. Dryden immediately touches on the fact that he is without a title but makes a virtue of it: he is 'nobler yet/In his own worth, and without Title great' (900–1). He is the antithesis of the 'meer Nobles'. He is a great exemplar of the 'conservative myth'; he has all the qualities of reason and control which are needed to prevent the wild energy of the malcontents from destroying all government. In retirement he smiles at the 'mad Labour' of his successors, those 'rasher Charioteers' in Parliament, who 'Misguide the Seasons and mistake the Way' (911). Like Phæton, Apollo's son, they fly too near the sun, and thereby endanger the state. The myth of Phæton fits nicely into the pattern of the conservative myth. Foolish mortals believe that by taking the reins of government they can fly nearer the sun without coming to harm. It is better to leave things to those who know the old paths which are the safest.

The King Speaks (933–1031)

Following the brief and cogent summary of the crisis (914–32), the poem rises to a truly heroic level. This is marked by the style. The first sentence has a structure typical of Miltonic and Virgilian epic: '... opprest, ... revolving ... his patience tir'd,/Thus ... *David* spoke' (933–7), the main subject and verb being reserved for the end of the sentence.

Some critics have found the poem's conclusion disappointing. Dr Johnson's assessment is worth quoting at length:

> As an approach to historical truth was necessary, the action and catastrophe were not in the poet's power; there is therefore an unpleasing disproportion between the beginning and the end. We are alarmed by a faction formed out of many sects ... while the king's friends are few and weak. The chiefs on either part are set forth to view; but when expectation is at the height the king makes a speech, and
> > *Henceforth a Series of new time began.*
>
> Who can forbear to think of an enchanted castle ... which vanishes at once into air when the destined knight blows his horn before it?

Johnson's point is that by faithfully following real history Dryden was forced to manufacture a dramatic conclusion from unfinished events. In view of the crisis facing the government, one might suppose that some-

Absalom and Achitophel: *A Commentary on the Poem*

thing more than a speech was needed to initiate 'a Series of new time'.

Several points can be made in answer to Johnson. First, the divine nature of the king is given great prominence:

> The God-like *David* spoke: with awfull fear
> His Train their Maker in their Master hear. (937–8)

It is hardly appropriate to compare this with a knight blowing his horn. Johnson was evidently not prepared to give much weight to Dryden's use of religious allegory, which tends to elevate merely historical events to the level of eternal truths. He saw only the events and not the myth of divine kingship. The king's speech, Johnson implies, has the air of a *deus ex machina* – the contrived divine intervention at the end of a classical play. In fact, Dryden's poetic strategy depended entirely on the power of the divine office of the king. Charles's 'God-like' role is hammered home. He resembles 'Godlike Kings' in defending his servants in distress. He asks the question 'Why am I forc'd, like Heaven, against my mind . . .?' Secondly, the speech is derived from actual political pamphlets (see p. 17), which had some real influence on the situation. Thirdly, Johnson underestimates Dryden's grasp of Charles's delaying tactics during the Exclusion Crisis. Secure in his legal powers (he is England's 'lawfull Lord') he indulges one of the prime virtues of his Maker – 'mercy':

> Thus long have I, by native mercy sway'd,
> My wrongs dissembl'd, my revenge delay'd: (939–40)

Charles has been pushed too far. Like God, he is a loving father, always willing to forgive, but sometimes he must be a wrathful God: 'Must I at length the Sword of Justice draw?' It is interesting to note that Charles makes it quite clear that his patience is a conscious strategy:

> Yet, since they will divert my Native course,
> 'Tis time to shew I am not Good by Force. (949–50)

In normal times a king's mercy and patience are sufficient to command obedience, but if malcontents fail to understand the king's full majesty, he must reveal it. Having turned their backs on Charles's 'Grace' (1007), they must now face his 'Law'. The king delays his counter-measures, and pretends to retreat, only to strike back when his enemies are at their weakest:

> Nor doubt th' event; for Factious crowds engage
> In their first Onset, all their Brutal Rage;
> Then, let 'em take an unresisted Course,
> Retire and Traverse [thwart], and Delude their Force: (1018–21)

Masterstudies: Absalom and Achitophel

Charles had been criticized for pardoning and commuting punishments. Parliament objected strongly in 1679 when Charles pardoned the Earl of Danby, following his impeachment. In 1680 he commuted the Catholic Lord Stafford's cruel sentence. Now the time for bolder action had come.

Those, who, like Dr Johnson, are unimpressed by Charles's assertion of authority, overlook the fact that the measures he took and was taking at the time of the poem's appearance were indeed effective in turning the tide. Harold Brooks has helpfully summarized the steps taken by Charles:

The counter-strokes are principally the dissolution of the Third Exclusion Parliament at Oxford on 28 March 1681, the resolve to proceed without summoning Parliament henceforth, and the judicial measures against Shaftesbury and his henchmen. These measures consisted primarily in the trial and execution, at Oxford, beyond the scope of a London jury, of Stephen College [an anti-Catholic agitator], and in the arrest of Shaftesbury himself.

One must add that none of this would have been possible had not Charles made a secret treaty (March 1681) with Louis XIV, in order to get three and a half million crowns over a period of three years. This enabled him to dissolve Parliament and throw off his financial dependency. His brother James had recommended this course of action, because it would 'enable him to dispense with parliament, and thereafter engage in "resolute counsels" ' (Ogg), although it should be noted that James had earlier adopted a more militant and potentially disastrous view of Charles's best course of action. Schilling's cynical remarks are not without truth: 'The patient man was patient until he was sure of having enough money so that he could afford to be furious.'

However specious Charles's exercise of authority appears to us, we must not forget that in these measures Charles was proceeding by due process of 'necessary Law' (1003). Dryden and other Tories sincerely believed that, by defending the king's prerogative against the Whig's attempts to prune it, they were upholding the crown's rightful role in the constitution (see p. 70). Dryden did not support absolutism, and the king is made to express a firmly constitutional view when he questions Parliament's right to determine the succession:

> A King's at least a part of Government,
> And mine as requisite as their Consent: (977–8)

It is probable that in his heart Charles would have considered even this formulation an invasion of his prerogative. His moderate tone is counterbalanced by the assertion of the monarch's right to rule (946). The word 'Law' appears five times and 'Lawfull' twice in the last forty lines of the poem, giving great prominence to the king's godlike role of arbiter of justice. In the end, the message is a simple one: a lawful monarch must assert his right to prevent a dangerous faction from excluding the rightful heir from the succession.

David is endowed with such dignity and divine authority that the reader easily forgets the king's weaknesses which were in part responsible for the situation. The poem's opening witty allusions to the king's licentiousness are now readily forgotten or placed in the divine perspective of the allegory. Dryden's achievement was to transform and enrich the potent conservative myth of kingship, order and loyalty by shaping it into a poem of elegant statement, delicate satire and pungent political debate. The fact that it did not succeed in influencing the outcome of Shaftesbury's trial did not in any way diminish its importance for literary tradition and for the conservative ideology of its time.

A Commentary on Part II

Background: The Medal

Shaftesbury was in the Tower of London for four months on a charge of high treason. A week after the appearance of *Absalom Part I* he was indicted at the Old Bailey, but the charge was dismissed. A jury packed with Whigs returned a verdict of 'Ignoramus' (i.e. lack of competence to judge). In the spring of 1682 a medal was struck for the Whigs by George Bower. On the obverse was a bust of Shaftesbury, and on the reverse a view of London Bridge and the Tower, with the sun breaking through a cloud. The inscriptions read 'Lætamur' (Let us rejoice) and '24 Nov. 1681'. Shaftesbury's supporters wore the medal on their lapels. Dryden's response, a poem called 'The Medal', appeared in the middle of March 1682, probably commissioned once again by Charles.

In this poem Dryden changes his satiric tactics and writes in the more virulent Juvenalian manner, abandoning the 'moderation' he had cultivated in the first *Absalom*. The acquittal of Shaftesbury evidently required a strong response. Images of heroic wickedness are replaced by images of corruption. Irony and humour are abandoned for abuse and indignation. The threat to government and order now seemed so imminent that the refinements of wit and subtle indirection had to be laid to one side. There remains the power and energy of vituperation, which Juvenal authorized in his most bitter early satires. The opening prose

Masterstudies: Absalom and Achitophel

'Epistle to the Whigs' differs significantly from the preface to the reader in the first *Absalom*. Shaftesbury is compared to Nero and Caligula, the cruel and inhuman Roman emperors of tradition. He declares with bitter humour that Shaftesbury's head 'would be seen to more advantage if it were placed on a spike of the Tower' (the regicides' bodies, including Cromwell's, were exhumed and treated in this fashion in 1660). He regards the striking of the medal as 'a piece of notorious impudence in the face of the established government'. He alludes to the Whigs' extra-Parliamentary agitation as seditious, and attacks the mass petitioning (see p. 79) of the king, arguing 'You are not the trustees of the public liberty'. He vilifies the recent Whig defence of Shaftesbury in *No Protestant Plot*, which he claims was inspired by Marvell's *Account of the Growth of Popery* (1677), a major 'Whig' political work. The supposed author was in fact Robert Ferguson (Judas in Part II, 320 ff.).

In the last part of the 'Epistle' Dryden invites his enemies to reply to his accusations: 'Rail at me abundantly; and, not to break with custom, do it without wit: by this method you will gain a considerable point, which is, wholly to waive the answer of my arguments . . . If God has not blest you with the talent of rhyming, make use of my poor stock and welcome.' There is a great deal of 'railing' in the poem, but, Dryden implies, his at least has 'wit' and 'talent'. Indeed, but for the skill of his writing there is little to distinguish Dryden's violence from that of his enemies. He repeats the arguments of *Absalom*, and uses the familiar anti-Puritan idiom ('canting', 'hypocritic zeal', 'fanatic', 'factions', 'saint', 'sects', 'Gospel-phrase'). He adds a rich brew of emotive metaphor. The Whig jury which acquitted Shaftesbury 'leech-like, lived on blood'; London is full of 'monsters . . . Engendered on the slime thou leav'st'; Shaftesbury's supporters 'Cyclops-like . . . Chop up a minister at every meal'; the nation is 'pox'd' by Shaftesburian infection; the preachers are drunk on 'fresh fumes of madness'. Dryden shows no restraint in his portrayal of Shaftesbury:

> But thou, the pander of the people's hearts,
> (O crooked soul, and serpentine in arts!)
> Whose blandishments a loyal land have whor'd,
> And broke the bonds she plighted to her lord;
> What curses on thy blasted name will fall!

The rather heroic Satanism of Achitophel is replaced by a more unpleasant image of the venomous serpent, of 'A vermin wriggling in the usurper's ear'. It is possible to admire the power of Dryden's vituperation, but there is little doubt that the literary appeal of such invective is

Absalom and Achitophel: *A Commentary on the Poem*

limited, even when it is so neatly phrased. His literary enemy Thomas Shadwell almost certainly wrote 'The Medal of John Bayes' (1682), a violent reply to 'The Medal', in which he sneeringly admits that Dryden 'has an easiness in rhyme, and a knack at versifying, and can make a slight thing seem pretty and clinquant'. Shadwell's attack on Dryden is as personal as anything in 'The Medal', though much less elegantly written. The flatness of Shadwell's style makes it seem more insulting. He defends both Monmouth and Shaftesbury and describes them as saviours of the nation and upholders of patriotic Protestantism. He accuses Dryden of libel and obscenity, and of slavishly fawning upon the 'Popish knaves'. He concludes:

> Now farewell wretched mercenary Bayes [Dryden was poet laureate],
> Who the King libell'd, and did Cromwell praise.
> Farewell, abandon'd rascal! only fit
> To be abus'd by thy own scurrilous wit.
> Which thou would'st do, and for a moderate sum,
> Answer thy *Medal*, and thy *Absalom*.

Shadwell is almost certainly taking revenge for Dryden's devastating mockery in *Mac Flecknoe* (written 1676). Dryden's poem was the first great mock-heroic poem of the Augustan age. The poem includes a mock-coronation in which Shadwell is to be crowned the monarch of dullness. Dryden brilliantly deploys all the resources of heroic verse to load Shadwell with a weight of incongruous brilliance under which he sinks into oblivion. Heroic grandeur is soiled by the ugly urban surroundings of the occasion. The streets of the city are strewn with the scattered pages of unsold authors:

> Now Empress Fame had published the renown
> Of Sh——'s coronation thro' the town.
> Rous'd by report of fame, the nations meet,
> From near Bunhill, and distant Watling-street.
> No Persian carpets spread th' imperial way,
> But scatter'd limbs of mangled poets lay;
> From dusty shops neglected authors come,
> Martyrs of pies, and relics of the bum.
> Much Heywood, Shirley, Ogleby there lay,
> But loads of Sh—— almost chok'd the way.

It was hardly surprising if this stung Shadwell. A war of insults continued sporadically. Shadwell's poem was not the last volley; Dryden had his revenge in *Absalom and Achitophel Part II*.

Masterstudies: Absalom and Achitophel

The Second Part of Absalom and Achitophel

Absalom Part II was published in November 1682 and reprinted shortly after with some corrections and alterations. It continues the story of Part I to May 1682. Nahum Tate, a friend of Dryden's, was responsible for the largest part of it. The publisher of the 1716 *Miscellany*, Tonson, attributed only lines 310–509 to Dryden, 'besides some touches in other places'. These touches have never been identified with any certainty. The Scott-Saintsbury edition of Dryden argues that the characters of Corah (69–102) and Arod (534–55), and the account of the Green Ribbon Club (522–33) are also by Dryden, but since these ascriptions are based purely on stylistic intuitions they cannot be taken as authoritative. Nahum Tate's poetic skills were of a much lower order than Dryden's. His tribute to Dryden (Asaph) near the end of the poem (1039–64) forecasts the lasting fame of the first *Absalom*:

> The Song of *Asaph* shall for ever last!
> With wonder late Posterity shall dwell
> On *Absalom*, and false *Achitophel*: (1042–4)

Tate's couplets lack Dryden's terseness and wit. He sustains the heroic manner set by Dryden in Part I, but often allows the grand manner to become empty and conventional. He throws in extended heroic similes and long-winded panegyrics of the king's supporters, scarcely keeping up the satiric framework at all. For example, in a passage referring to the Duke of York's exile to Brussels in 1679, Tate uses Edmund Waller's panegyric style:

> Go injur'd Heroe while propitious Gales,
> Soft as thy Consorts breath inspire thy Sails [etc.] (617–18)

The poem's structure is less rich than the first *Absalom*'s: the narrative is undramatic, the speeches lack tension, and the characterization is flat, with the exception of Dryden's own.

The poem culminates in a panegyric on James in celebration of his return to London on 7 May, three weeks after his shipwreck on the *Gloucester*. The hero of this piece of formal flattery is much less vividly portrayed than the 'Godlike' David of *Absalom I*. This is not the only difference in emphasis between the first and second parts. There are signs that material written for the earlier poem was rejected because it did not fit its moderate tone, but was included in Part II because it suited its more unbridled fury. Howard Schless rightly argued that 'The first *Absalom* is a poem of persuasion; the second, a poem of attack.'

Absalom and Achitophel: *A Commentary on the Poem*

SUMMARY OF AND BRIEF COMMENTARY ON PART II

1–114

The style and themes of *Absalom I* are recapitulated and the situation is brought up to date. Absalom retains popular support. Tate keeps up Dryden's anti-democratic rhetoric: 'pamper'd crowds', 'giddy Rabble', 'Villain Herd', 'Rascle Rabble'. Next Tate describes the continued attacks on the queen (Michal) and Titus Oates's (Corah's) endless spinning out of the Popish Plot. But worst are the 'viler crew' who, with Achitophel, sustain the 'Good old Cause' and aim to bring down the king's brother, James.

115–275

As in *Absalom I* the second section of the poem is an exchange of speeches between Absalom and Achitophel. However, the political situation in 1682 was much less favourable to Shaftesbury, and this is reflected in Absalom's serious doubts and questionings. The exchanges are much less dramatic than Dryden's; there is no longer a parallel with the temptation scenes of *Paradise Lost*. Absalom now sees that the plot is being used for political ends and doubts the legitimacy of aiming at the throne. Like Macbeth, his mind is seriously divided: the deed, bad in imagination, will be much worse if committed. If he opposes the actual murder of the king, he himself might well be the next victim. He sees through the 'Pretence of Public Good'. Achitophel replies with another argument of Macbeth's: you are so far in now, you have no choice but to press on. Absalom accuses Achitophel of inconsistency. As the king's minister he had been hard on 'property' and had argued for absolutism. Once disgraced he changes his coat and argues against absolutism on behalf of property! One can say that this is a travesty of the historical events which led to Shaftesbury's adoption of the Whig causes. Achitophel acknowledges that his actions are governed by self-interest, but advocates continuation of the struggle, through Parliament, to exclude James. With hindsight we can see that Parliament had no chance of success while Charles was in receipt of Louis's subsidies.

276–555 (310–509 is by Dryden)

This section surveys the king's enemies, extending the briefer account in *Absalom I*. They include Sir Robert Clayton (Ishban), a Whig MP and Lord Mayor; Sir Thomas Player (Rabsheka), a Whig MP who had encouraged belief in the plot; several dissenters: Robert Ferguson (Judas), James Forbes (Phaleg), and Samuel Johnson (Ben-Jochanan);

Masterstudies: Absalom and Achitophel

other Whig writers: Samuel Pordage (Mephibosheth), Elkanah Settle (Doeg), and Thomas Shadwell (Og); and Sir William Waller (Arod), a magistrate and persecutor of Catholics.

556–724
Taking up the narrative, Tate describes the continued hostility of Parliament, James's departure for Brussels (he includes a fulsome panegyric on James), the religious and political fears of the populace. He argues that there was no reason to fear Louis XIV's intentions, and laments the divisive effects of Louis's bribery of the Whigs. At all costs a new civil war must be avoided. Dryden always showed a much shrewder grasp of Louis's policies, which included the neutralization of England; he saw clearly that Louis would always be willing to stir up trouble but not to support Charles in any overt fashion ('Foment the war, but not support the King').

725–830
Echoing *Absalom I,* Tate celebrates the revival of the king's fortunes. David asserts his authority, and his brother returns from exile to popular acclaim. Tate's praises hardly accord with the historical record. James had been royal commissioner in Scotland, and by all accounts had proved vengeful and mean-minded.

831–930
The final exchange between Absalom and Achitophel marks a clear rift between them. While Absalom sees support for him slipping away, he is unwilling to be persuaded into reckless measures by Achitophel, who desperately casts around for 'Some new Pretender'. Tate addresses Absalom directly ('Wake Absalom . . .') and tries to reason him out of any further treasonous thoughts; even if successful, he will ultimately be betrayed by 'Faction', and live to see the undoing of 'Monarchy it self'.

931–1064
Tate surveys in leisurely fashion the king's supporters, in an attempt to complete Dryden's list of honour. His list is distinctly nostalgic, and includes a number of superannuated royalist heroes including General Monck (Abdael), Arlington (Eliab), Lord Chancellor Finch (Amri), and Robert L'Estrange (Sheva), the notorious controller of royal censorship.

1065–1130
Tate inserts here a sombre passage equivalent to Dryden's on Ossory

Absalom and Achitophel: *A Commentary on the Poem*

(see p. 45). It describes the wreck of James's ship, the *Gloucester*, on its way to fetch his wife from Scotland. Once again the historical record hardly supports Tate's eulogistic treatment of James. He tells (1097–8) of James's selfless sorrow for 'such Followers lost'. David Ogg reports that 'contemporaries attributed to him an undue solicitude for his priests, his dogs and his treasure while the ship was sinking.' Of course one must allow for the possible Whig prejudices of Ogg's sources! The mood changes once more as Tate celebrates the glorious return of James and his duchess.

1131–40

The last few lines echo the conclusion of *Absalom I* by leaving the king centre stage in full command. The pretext for this victory may seem rather flimsy: Sir James Moore, Lord Mayor of London, precipitates a period of political in-fighting which results in the defeat of the Whigs in London. In fact, control of London was of vital importance to the king's strategy. As we have seen in *Absalom I*, packing of juries by the Whigs was a thorn in the side of the government. The final couplet is a clear echo of Dryden's conclusion:

> With *David* then was *Israel's* Peace restor'd,
> Crowds Mournd their Errour and Obey'd their Lord. (1139–40)

Dryden concluded *Absalom I* with:

> Once more the Godlike *David* was Restor'd,
> And willing Nations knew their Lawfull Lord.

COMMENTARY ON LINES 310–509 (BY DRYDEN)

Dryden's lines are part of the long section of negative satire against the supporters of Shaftesbury and the Whig cause. They are unusual in two ways. First, they include the only *literary* satire in the two poems. Secondly, they are much more personally insulting than most of the characterizations in *Absalom I*. The Whig attacks on the earlier poem and on 'The Medal' evidently stung Dryden into an uncharacteristic violence of style.

310–99: 'Priests without Grace'

These lines attack Dissenters who sell their pens for money. First, there is Robert Ferguson (Judas), known as 'the Plotter', originally a Presbyterian minister, ejected in 1662 in accordance with the Act of Uniformity. Dryden wickedly links him with Judas Iscariot, the apostles'

Masterstudies: Absalom and Achitophel

steward, whom he probably conflates with Judas of Galilee, a leader of a popular revolt in 6 A.D. Ferguson became chaplain to Monmouth and encouraged him in thoughts of rebellion. Bishop Burnet's contemporary portrait of Ferguson resembles Dryden's. Burnet thought him 'a hot and a bold man, whose spirit was naturally turned to plotting'. The 'College' referred to in line 325 was established in Islington by Ferguson for Nonconformists. Phaleg is traditionally identified as James Forbes, another Scottish clergyman, who 'Struts it like a Patriot'. The anti-Scottish chauvinism is a common feature of Augustan satires, and appears, for example, in the poems of Charles Churchill in the 1760s. The Scots Covenanters had been a thorn in the side of the English ever since 1637 when Archbishop Laud's decision to impose the Book of Common Prayer on Scotland sparked off the movement and precipitated the Civil Wars. Scotland was kept under control during the interregnum and Charles II's reign, and was finally united with England in 1707. The Rev. Samuel Johnson (Ben-Jochanan) became chaplain to Lord Russell, the Whig leader in the Commons, and wrote against the doctrine of passive obedience in *Julian the Apostate* (1682), in which he argued that the primitive Christians rightly opposed the efforts of the pagan emperor Julian to remove Christianity as the established religion. This would seem to justify the Whigs' attempts to prevent the ousting of Protestant Christianity by excluding James. Dryden attacks the book in lines 371–91, ridiculing the idea that the primitive Christians' resistance to tyranny justified the belief that 'Saints own no Allegiance to their Prince' (381). For this book and others Johnson was fined, imprisoned, pilloried and whipped.

The portraits of Forbes and Johnson contain two favourite targets of Augustan satire: hypocritical sexual misdemeanours and writing for money. The lines accusing Forbes of cuckolding his employer are typical of Dryden's mock-heroic style:

> Can dry Bones Live? Or *Skeletons* produce
> The Vital Warmth of Cuckoldizing Juice?
> Slim *Phaleg* cou'd, and at the Table fed,
> Return'd the gratefull product to the Bed. (338–41)

The first line echoes the passage on God's resurrection of dry bones in Ezekiel 37:2–10. The second line retains the lofty style in its obscene reference to a cuckolder's sperm ('Cuckoldizing Juice'). Dryden was a master of dignified dirt-throwing! The stately third and fourth lines describe how Phaleg is fed at his master's table only in order to give him energy to have intercourse with his master's wife. Forbes was in fact beaten (see line 344) by the order of the Earl of Derby whom he served,

Absalom and Achitophel: *A Commentary on the Poem*

but there is no evidence to suggest that Dryden correctly named the cause. The apparently heartless accusation that a man writes only because he is short of money goes back to classical satire and should be regarded as a satiric metaphor, at least in part. The Augustans were fond of the jibe, because it fitted neatly with their anti-Puritan rhetoric. Passing over 'famish'd *Phaleg*', who talks 'Treason for his daily Bread' (350–1), Dryden turns to Ben Jochanan whose career is described as motivated purely by material needs:

> A *Jew* of humble Parentage was He,
> By Trade a *Levite*, though of low Degree:
> His Pride no higher than the Desk aspir'd,
> But for the Drudgery of Priests was hir'd
> To Reade and Pray in Linen Ephod brave,
> And pick up single *Sheckles* from the Grave.
> Married at last, and finding Charge come faster,
> He cou'd not live by God, but chang'd his Master:
> Inspir'd by Want, was made a Factious Tool,
> They Got a Villain, and we lost a Fool. (354–63)

Notice the careful emphases in the words 'humble', 'Trade', 'low Degree', 'no higher', 'Drudgery', 'hir'd', 'pick up single *Sheckles*', 'Want'. The classical and humanist spirit underlying this mode of satire suggests that nothing great can be done for a mercenary motive, that lowly parentage inclines a person to narrow horizons, that writers of high principle are above corruption, and that people who write for money are often incompetent. Dryden is cleverly able to imply that Johnson's Whiggish *Julian* was written only to feed his growing family (360–2). Line 363 neatly clinches the argument by suggesting that Whigs ('They') have gained a 'Villain', while the court ('we') has got rid of a 'Fool'.

400–509: 'Slaves in metre' (*Doeg and Og*)

Having disposed of the Whig clergy Dryden turns to the Whig poetasters, describing them in openly insulting terms as

> Poor Slaves in metre, dull and adle-pated,
> Who Rhime below ev'n *David*'s Psalms translated. (402–3)

The worst insult an Augustan satirist could level against a writer was that he was worse than Thomas Sternhold and John Hopkins were in their metrical version of the Psalms (completed in 1562). The three writers attacked in the lines which follow all took up the pen against Dryden's Tory poems. Samuel Pordage (Mephibosheth) wrote *Azaria and Hushai* (1682); Elkanah Settle (Doeg) wrote *Absalom Senior: or, Achitophel*

Masterstudies: Absalom and Achitophel

Transpros'd (1682); and Thomas Shadwell (Og) almost certainly wrote *The Medal of John Bayes* (see above).

Doeg The attack on Settle is reminiscent of *Mac Flecknoe* and no less insulting. Settle had a great success in 1667 with *Cambyses King of Persia*, which he wrote while still a student. He threatened to rival Dryden, who then ruled the stage with his heroic plays. Settle enjoyed the patronage of Rochester, who openly set him up in opposition to Dryden as a playwright. His famous heroic play *The Empress of Morocco* (1673) drew the insults of Dryden, Shadwell and John Crowne (who succeeded Settle in Rochester's favour) in *Notes and Observations on The Empress of Morocco* (1674). Recruited by Shaftesbury in London, he became in effect the Whig poet laureate (the 'City Poet') in direct rivalry with Dryden, who was the official Poet Laureate. His career in support of the Whigs culminated in his appointment in 1680, during the Popish Plot furore, as organizer-in-chief of the pope-burning procession held on the anniversary of Queen Elizabeth's birthday (17 November). In *The Character of a Popish Successor* (1681) he urged the exclusion of James. Settle deserted the Whigs for the Tories in 1683, when he saw the king was winning, but switched back to the Whigs in 1688 when James II was about to fall. His duncehood was immortalized in Alexander Pope's *The Dunciad*.

In *Absalom Senior*, Settle accused Dryden of turning his coat from self-interest, switching from 'commonwealth's man' to 'royalist' with ease. He attributes Dryden's anti-clerical views to his disappointed ambition to become a priest, and specifically his failure to secure the post of Provost to Eton College. Dryden's description of Doeg is a classic piece of dunce-baiting:

> *Doeg*, though without knowing how or why,
> Made still a blund'ring kind of Melody;
> Spurd boldly on, and Dash'd through Thick and Thin,
> Through Sense and Non-sense, never out nor in;
> Free from all meaning, whether good or bad,
> And in one word, Heroically mad . . . (412–17)

Interestingly, Settle, Shadwell and Pordage all grudgingly acknowledged Dryden's literary skill and concentrated their attacks on its application to unworthy ends, while Dryden dismissed them totally as writers. Dryden and Pope excelled in this mock-heroic literary satire, which culminates in the eighteenth-century writings of the Scriblerus Club (a Tory group of writers including Pope, Jonathan Swift and John Gay).

Absalom and Achitophel: *A Commentary on the Poem*

Pope's *The Dunciad* is the masterpiece of this genre. Even the lines quoted above contain links with both Dryden's *Mac Flecknoe* and Pope's *Dunciad*, as the following quotations show:

> [Flecknoe was] Through all the realms of Non-sense, absolute.
> ....
> The rest to some faint meaning make pretence,
> But *Shadwell* never deviates into sense.
> (*Mac Flecknoe*, 6, 19–20)

In *The Dunciad* the Goddess of Dulness invites the dunces to compete at mud-diving (a metaphor for dirty writing) in the Thames: 'Here prove who best can dash through thick and thin' (II.276).

Dryden is able to be less abusive than his enemies, because his sense of serene superiority as a writer lifts him above the mundane and purely personal level. What Ian Jack says of *Mac Flecknoe* can also be said of the portraits of Doeg and Og: 'The reader enjoys hearing Shadwell being abused without feeling that he is assisting in an unmannerly brawl; and the elevation of the verse adds authority to the condemnation.' The condescension of 'Made still a blund'ring kind of Melody' is deeply insulting without being coarse or violent. The neo-classical values of 'decorum' and elegant good sense (see p. 82) licensed a good deal of snobbish dismissiveness and social superiority in the name of literary values. It is fascinating to see, nevertheless, how Dryden can, despite his neo-classical poise, get away with being quite obscene, for example in the analogy developed in lines 437–40, which was inspired by a ribald Cavalier ballad of 1647.

Once again a Whig writer's mercenary motives are pilloried. Settle's satires are feeble, because writing to him is a 'trade' conducted in a 'garret'. He will do anything for a bite to eat:

> For Almonds he'll cry Whore to his own Mother:
> And call Young *Absalom* King *David*'s Brother. (429–30)

As is often the case, Dryden's imagery has specific literary resonances. The reference to almonds is from proverbial literature about parrots and almonds. Shakespeare, for example, uses the proverb in *Troilus and Cressida*, V, ii, 193: 'the parrot will not do more for an almond than he for a commodious drab.' The other half of Dryden's line was corroborated in 1683 by an anonymous writer who declared that Settle had let it be known that 'his Mother was a Whore'. The point about Settle calling James 'Absalom' is a reference to Settle's *Absalom Senior*. Dryden's references to Settle's rather plebeian activities in London

Masterstudies: Absalom and Achitophel

(organizing a firework display for the Whigs and writing drolls – see lines 251 ff.) contribute to the general picture of vulgarity and middle-class tastelessness. However, the prevailing theme is Settle's incompetence as a writer. A standard insult in Augustan satire is that one's enemy is too intellectually feeble to have any impact as a satirist:

> Spightfull he is not, though he wrote a Satyr,
> For still there goes some *thinking* to ill-Nature: (421–2)

Rochester's earlier attack on Sir Carr Scroope in 'On Poet Ninny' makes the same point: 'But never satire did so softly bite'. Rochester may have taken this idea from Dryden who, in *Mac Flecknoe*, wrote of Shadwell: 'Thy inoffensive satires never bite.' However, the metaphor was a traditional one, used, for example, by Milton when he mocks the Elizabethan satirist Joseph Hall for calling the first three books of his satires 'Toothless'; Milton declares that you might as well say 'toothless teeth'! The essential point is that true satire should be incisive. Dryden adds a further insult by suggesting that Settle's abuse of others is not a literary talent but 'mere instinct' which helps him to convert prose into verse: 'For to write Verse with him is to *Transprose*.' (444) Dryden here cleverly reapplies a term once used against him in *The Rehearsal*, in which he is called 'Bayes' (a bay leaf crown was traditionally a symbol of literary renown), and boasts of his ability to change verse into prose and vice versa. One character declares: 'Methinks, Mr Bayes, that putting verse into prose should be called transprosing.'

Og The portrait of Og is the most exuberant and inventive passage in Part II. Dryden had already devoted his superb *Mac Flecknoe* to mocking Shadwell as a writer. It was published in 1682, long after it was composed, and was obviously intended to be read as part of the Whig-Tory war, because the editor seems to have added the sub-title 'Upon the True-Blew-Protestant Poet, T[homas] S[hadwell]'. This is highly misleading, since only Shadwell's role as poet is attacked. Also, the political label fitted Shadwell in 1682, but would not have done in 1676. The Og portrait is different in being a much more personal satire. There had been a continuous though not especially hostile debate between Dryden and Shadwell since 1668 about Ben Jonson's drama. Shadwell resented Dryden's reasoned criticisms of Jonson, believed that Jonson's comedy of 'humours' was still relevant to the Restoration stage, and denigrated Dryden's preference for the more modern comedy of witty repartee. In his article on the date of *Mac Flecknoe* David Vieth draws attention to the fact that the poem makes no reference to any of Shadwell's writings

Absalom and Achitophel: *A Commentary on the Poem*

after July 1676, when his popular *The Virtuoso* was published with a preface highly critical of Dryden's views on comedy. Shadwell's apparent inability to grasp Dryden's distinction between the modern and the older senses of 'wit' must have seemed to Dryden evidence of duncehood.

Shadwell's career as a dramatist is much more impressive than Dryden's portraits would lead one to expect. He wrote at least eighteen plays between 1668 and his early death at fifty in 1692. They included a comedy of humours (*The Sullen Lovers*, 1668, his first play), wit comedies in the modern manner of Etherege and Wycherley (*Epsom Wells*, 1673, is the best known), heroic plays (*The Libertine*, 1676, is impressive), sentimental middle-class comedies (*The Squire of Alsatia*, 1688), and spectacular operatic plays (*The Tempest*, 1674, adapted from Shakespeare's play, was the most successful). Even though he kept up with the fashion, Shadwell belonged to a new class of professional writers whose middle-class moral values emerge even in his most exuberant work. Some of the contempt expressed by Dryden and others against the Whig writers was directed towards their humble origins and bourgeois aspirations. However, it is interesting to note that the true (if unorthodox) aristocrat the Earl of Rochester had a higher opinion of Shadwell's talent. In 'An Allusion to Horace', he questions Dryden's critical judgements, but praises Shadwell's natural ability:

> Shadwell's unfinished works do yet impart
> Great proofs of force of nature, none of art.
> With just, bold strokes he dashes here and there,
> Showing great mastery with little care . . .

The neo-classical Dryden could never admire the virtues of energy unless they were combined with artistic care. The rakish Rochester was able to rise above such niceness. He took an aristocratic delight in the vulgar world of the bourgeoisie, as his poem 'Timon' reveals. Likewise, he saw both Shadwell's lack of polish *and* his vitality. Pope follows Dryden in treating middle-class energy as frenzied and mindless.

Dryden's opening description of Og is openly offensive in its physical directness. The image of the portly poet had already been used to good advantage in a passage of *Mac Flecknoe* in which Flecknoe, Shadwell's poetic father, compares his son to Jonson:

> Nor let thy mountain belly make pretence
> Of likeness; thine's a tympany of sense.
> A tun of man in thy large bulk is writ,
> But sure thou'rt but a kilderkin of wit. (193–6)

Masterstudies: Absalom and Achitophel

Both Jonson and Shadwell were fat, but Shadwell's large belly sounds like a hollow drum and symbolizes his emptiness and lack of sense. His bulk ('tun') is contrasted to the size of his wit (a 'kilderkin' is much smaller than a 'tun' and verbally is a diminutive; compare 'manikin'). The portrait of Og dwells more continuously and offensively on Shadwell's bulk, and the associations evoked are much more damaging. The biblical Og was famous for his size (Deuteronomy 3:11). In the poem his 'tun of Midnight-work' rolls home from a 'Treason Tavern', home of the Whigs' Green Ribbon Club, where we assume he has been engaged in anti-government talk. The next couplet paints a gleeful picture:

> Round as a Globe, and Liquor'd ev'ry chink,
> Goodly and Great he Sayls behind his Link [torch-bearer]; (460–1)

But any impression of harmless and sublime inebriation is firmly suppressed in the following lines which describe his 'Bulk' as 'A Monstrous mass of foul corrupted matter', made by 'Devils'. This linking of Shadwell with the powers of evil is of course metaphorical, but nevertheless deeply damning. Dryden continues:

> When wine has given him courage to Blaspheme,
> He Curses God, but God before Curst him; (466–7)

The concise wit of the second line is typical of Dryden's skill at effective insult. The drunken poet utters blasphemies against God, but, Dryden argues, his disgusting corpulence shows that God has cursed him in advance. God also showed his disapproval by making him poor, which was sensibly done. Why give him money to buy rich food ('Quail and Pheasant') when he vomits up even cheap fare ('Tripe and Carrion')? The traditional idea that a poet is born not made is turned to advantage: Shadwell 'never was a Poet of God's making' (475). The midwife prophesied his dullness. The reference to opium (482) is to the addiction that ultimately killed Shadwell. All warning is in vain; Shadwell persists in writing his 'Treason botcht in Rhime' (485). Dryden adds a final twist to the insult by suggesting that the treason is the least serious offence:

> A double Noose thou on thy Neck dost pull,
> For Writing Treason, and for Writing dull;
> To die for Faction is a Common evil,
> But to be hang'd for Non-sense is the Devil. (496–9)

The second part of *Absalom* is worth reading because it gives us a view of a different side of Dryden's satiric technique. In the first poem he had shown the skills of delicate irony, humour and mock-heroic grandeur. In the second poem he uses a more virulent and personal style of insult, calculated to serve the needs of the less favourable political situation following the acquittal of Shaftesbury. The comparison reminds us just how sensitive to the immediate occasion writers had to be in this period, and how they had to call on every possible stylistic resource to meet the demands of the moment. None did it with such panache as Dryden.

3 The Contexts of *Absalom and Achitophel*

T. S. Eliot once remarked that the English Civil War of the seventeenth century was still being fought. What did he mean? The divisions which emerged so catastrophically in 1641 concerned politics, religion and economic power. Some historians believe that the civil strife, which led to the execution of Charles I in 1649, was connected with the rise of the middle classes, whose new financial power was not reflected in political or religious structures. Others place greater emphasis upon the religious conflicts between the state religion, with its rich and powerful bishops, and those who regarded themselves as the upholders of the true Protestant faith against the dangerously Popish tendencies of Archbishop Laud's Anglican regime. Again, others believe that the wars started more or less by accident and not as a result of definable causes. Whatever the causes, the divisions left an indelible mark on English society. Despite the consciously cultivated ethos of 'common sense' and 'moderation' which prevailed after the restoration of the monarchy in 1660, the conflict between the interests of the court and the merchant classes, between Anglicans and Dissenters, between Tories and Whigs (from the 1670s), continued even beyond the momentous Revolution of 1688, which brought in a form of what we now call constitutional monarchy, under which the voice of the people (or rather part of it) was given primacy, although William of Orange was by no means the mere cipher that Shaftesbury was looking for in Monmouth.

One might argue that the recent conflict between 'wets' and 'dries' in the Conservative Governments of 1979 and 1983 are a repetition of the old conflicts between those who believe in tradition, stability and paternalistic government, and those who believe that a free market economy and private property are the foundation of all positive political values. Dryden, spokesman for the 'wet' Tory view, damns the 'dry' Whigs in no uncertain terms:

> By these the Springs of Property were bent,
> And wound so high, they Crack'd the Government. (499 500)

The merchant classes, argues Dryden, serve their own material interests and not the 'public good'. He sneers at the Puritan work ethic, their parsimony and their uncultured ways. He would have been surprised to find that in the 1980s such hard-edged attitudes were espoused by a so-called Tory party. He would have thought that the world had turned upside down!

In the following sections on the contexts of *Absalom* it is important to remember that they are central to the poem's meaning and not just 'background' material for rapid survey. This must always be remembered when a literary work is to be set in its historical context, but is especially important in the case of a political satire. Many critics have admired the poem but have relegated it to a level below poems such as *Paradise Lost* or *The Prelude*, not just on grounds of length, but because they feel that great poetry must transcend its time more thoroughly than Dryden's poem appears to do. There is a common view that poems on certain subjects – scientific (Lucretius's *On the Nature of Things*), theological (Dante's *Divine Comedy*), or political (*Absalom*) – have to work harder to become real poetry. If they succeed, it is then possible to include them in the canon of 'great poetry', which can be read by all readers in all periods. What this view tends to forget is that if we cut a poem or play or novel adrift from its context, we may gain some peculiarly modern perspective on it, but at the expense of *reducing* or even *distorting* its meanings and possible richness. It is probably impossible to reconstruct the full complexity of such contexts, and equally impossible to avoid imposing our own modern meanings on earlier writings, but the fact remains that we can approach a full and convincing interpretation only if we bring into focus not just a poem's purely literary qualities but also the living fabric of the real world in which the poem was born and from which it derived much of its energy. The poem is as much part of that world as it is separable from it. The following sections provide some of the elements of its 'world', in which it was immersed and to which it refers with unselfconscious ease.

The Economic and Social Context

It has proved difficult to reach an agreed account of the social and economic developments which led to the Industrial Revolution in this country. However, there is little doubt that the defeat of the royalist forces during the Civil Wars marked a crucial stage in a long process of change which finally saw the displacement of a feudal system by a modern capitalist one. By 1688 (the final defeat of the older royalism) 'trade' (maritime and commercial) had taken the place of religion as the pivot of international relations. There was a gradual but decisive shift towards a belief in free trade and the need to abolish governmental restrictions upon it. E. Lipson's account of the changes ushered in by the Civil Wars is helpful. He shows that the revolt against traditional authority in religion and government weakened the crown's economic authority. With the Restoration there was no revival of traditions which enabled the monarchy to prevent or penalize enclosures, promote the education of artisans, assess wages, require magistrates to provide work for the poor and so on. Lipson argues that 'As the outcome of the Great Rebellion the movement towards *laissez-faire* acquired increasing momentum. In the relaxation of state control lies the economic significance of the Civil War.' After the Restoration restrictive guild and apprentice regulations were weakened or ignored. However, as is the case with most important historical shifts the seeds of change were there at a much earlier stage.

In the century before the Civil Wars there was a dramatic price inflation, which had a serious effect on most classes and especially the poorest. At the end of the sixteenth century it was necessary to introduce poor laws and vagrancy laws to control the growth of roaming bands of landless men and women who had been thrown out of employment or small holdings partly as a result of the increasing pace of enclosure (the enforced consolidation of small-holdings into larger units for sheep pasturage, and later for arable farming). There were frequent proclamations against enclosure, but finally in 1624 Parliament recognized that enclosure was inevitable for the sake of economic progress, and in particular to achieve self-sufficiency in food. Modernized farming methods and new financial speculation resulted in deep changes in custom and tradition. Some of the older aristocracy floundered while others joined the craze for 'improvement'. Both Elizabeth and James I tried in vain to encourage gentry and aristocracy to return to the old days of 'hospitality' when the labourer and the peasant were protected in hard times by the lord of the manor's beneficence. Most significant of all, though modern historians disagree about it, there was a shift in the ownership of land away from the aristocracy toward the gentry. It is certainly possible to say that the House of Commons, which represented gentry (and some aristocracy) was growing in strength as a result of these changes at the expense of the House of Lords, although one cannot ignore the fact that the division of Commons and Lords was not strictly according to rank (many lords had great influence within the Commons).

During this period too there was a general and very large increase in industry. By 1640, for example, England produced three times as much coal as the rest of Europe put together. This and many other new

The Contexts of Absalom and Achitophel

industries required a considerable *capital investment*. Gradually, London became important as a financial centre, and its merchants provided loans and acted as middle-men for industry, for the smaller less-capitalized industries (cloth), and for overseas development (privateering). By the beginning of the Civil Wars most of the richest men in the land were City men and not the landed aristocracy. Parliament represented the City and the gentry against the power of the king and church. During the wars the power of London proved a vital factor in Parliament's victory over the king. It must be said at once that both sides were equally determined to suppress any democratic demands from below. Unrest among the poor was always a cause for alarm.

Among the immediate economic causes of the Civil Wars was the resistance to Charles I's continued interference in the economy. The royal coffers often had to be replenished by the sale of monopolies to courtiers whose financial killings aroused deserved hostility from the commercial classes. By 1621 there were said to be 700 of them! Conflict between king and Parliament over monopolies was a continuing problem before 1640. The industrial revolution of the nineteenth century would never have been possible without the victory of Parliament over such restrictive economic practices.

Traditional ways were further disrupted during the Civil Wars and the subsequent Commonwealth, mainly as a result of the massive sequestration of royalist and church lands, as well as huge financial levies and taxation. The new owners tended to exploit the land more ruthlessly and efficiently. Those royalists who 'compounded' and regained their estates tended to devote themselves to estate management rather than return to older, extravagant ways. The land settlement at the Restoration left many royalists without their lands. Others were either seriously impoverished or driven to emulate the tougher financial accounting of their enemies. Parliament, however, was determined to prevent lower-class attempts to win security for humbler occupiers of land (copyholders). They left the way open for the fullest economic exploitation of the land, unhampered by court or by the ordinary people. Efforts by the Diggers, for example, to take over common land for cultivation were defeated.

The Long Parliament abolished monopolies, but allowed the rich London merchant companies to retain their privileges, which often amounted to monopolistic powers. A bold attempt, led by the Levellers at the start of the Commonwealth, to introduce a more democratic control of the companies failed.

The restoration of the monarchy in 1660 saw no return to the older economic ways; there was no revival of monopolies or the royal

Masterstudies: Absalom and Achitophel

'prerogative courts' which had forced taxation upon the subject in the reign of Charles I. The king was now forced to go to Parliament for regular subsidies to cover his expenditure. Throughout his reign Charles II tried to establish an independent control over his income, and even resorted to secret agreements with Louis XIV in exchange for subsidies. Industry gradually began to flourish after the shocks of the plague, the Fire of London and the defeats in the naval wars against the Dutch in the 1660s (in the long-term England attained supremacy as a naval power, especially under William after 1688). With economic development there came a growing differentiation between the classes, and a steady increase in the number of landless workers who depended on wage-labour, while the number of more independent smallholders and yeomen declined. Industrial unrest in the towns gave rise to the new phenomenon – the 'mob'. From the point of view of all the ruling classes, whether aristocrats or gentry or merchants, the mass of working people were a necessary evil; the 'many-headed monster' was always associated with instability and disorder. We know very little of the common people's point of view, since most accounts come from those who so often despised them. (Apart from the remarkable outburst of popular writing during the Civil Wars, popular culture survives sparsely, in ballads, etc.)

Political Theory

Even though politics is prominent in his life and work, Dryden's political ideas could not be described as rigorous or systematic. A good part of his thinking was pragmatic and instinctive (which is not to say that it cannot be defined). In this he was in harmony with his king, whose political strengths stemmed from his pragmatic and undogmatic disposition. The Restoration settlement was itself highly unsystematic: the king's Declaration of Breda (April 1660) spoke in very general terms of a 'perfect union' of the people, and the 're-settlement of our [the monarch's] just rights and theirs [the people's] in a free Parliament'. Everyone seemed agreed that the sufferings of the nation now called for a 'limited' monarchy. While parliamentarians and royalists alike paid lip-service to this ideal, the king was clearly bent on a more absolutist path, if he could achieve it. The lack of clear definitions of the balance of government inevitably created a crisis when the king exceeded his legal power. There was no legal way to coerce him, and Parliament was driven to measures which the royalists regarded as unconstitutional, in order to assert its rights. The Exclusion Crisis demanded that Dryden reassert the justification for the king's preeminence in the constitution. As Isabel

Rivers has argued, 'Dryden is sure not so much of his theoretical position as of his practical responses to a specific situation.' What mattered was that the king's authority should be upheld and that all steps should be taken to avoid the excesses of absolutism and popular government. This 'moderation' was in reaction to the ferment of ideas and events of the previous generation.

Between 1620 and 1660 there was an outburst of political writings in England, some trying to provide theoretical justification for Charles I's desire to be an absolute monarch, some inspired by resistance to monarchy, and some reflecting the more down-to-earth political thinking which arose from the growing scientific and sceptical outlook of the period.

It is probable that the growth of science had the profoundest effect on political theory. Marlowe's *Dr Faustus* showed how the pride of human learning led to the most appalling blasphemy. While Marlowe's attitude towards Faustus's desire for unlimited knowledge was a complicated one, there was no doubt about Francis Bacon's. In the *Advancement of Learning* (1605) he took the momentous step of separating religion and the study of nature, so that there was no longer a need to fear that the desire for knowledge of God's creation was sinful. However, once man became free to inquire into the fundamentals of nature, certain other disturbing questions arose. Among them was the question – what foundation is there in a king's claim to be God's representative on earth? The demystification of nature also pointed to the demystification of kingship. The idea of the divine right of kings went with a belief in God's direct intervention in the course of history. The Baconian philosophy of science was closely related to the work of men such as Sir Walter Raleigh who began to study history, not as a reflection of God's purposes, but as human events and actions. In contrast, during the Civil Wars the Puritans (especially the Presbyterians, but also, notably, Cromwell) held to a providential view of history. At the Restoration Samuel Butler mocked this attitude unmercifully in *Hudibras*. The growing separation of the secular from the divine invited human beings to apply their unaided reason to fundamental questions of politics. Nothing could be more dangerous from the point of view of traditional thought. Dryden, himself a member of the 'Baconian' Royal Society, relied heavily on a biblical view of history (see p. 98) to preserve something of the mystique of kingship in a period inclined to more rational explanations of the universe.

Masterstudies: Absalom and Achitophel

Hobbes

The most original and influential work of political theory of the mid-century was undoubtedly Thomas Hobbes's *Leviathan* (1651), which broke radically with theocentric theories by making its starting point a materialistic analysis of human behaviour and psychology rather than a theological foundation. He begins by announcing that life is just 'motion of the limbs' caused by impulses from the heart (which is merely a 'spring') and the joints (which are 'so many wheels'). Life is continued motion; death is the cessation of motion. We fear death and therefore seek only to sustain our vital motion. Our moral sense is based entirely upon this natural desire. In the hypothetical 'state of nature', before any civilized society, we can have no security, because we continually fear that others will attack, rob or kill us. The only form of government which can provide us with the security we need is some form of absolute power capable of preventing men from preying upon one another. An absolute monarchy, for example, is able to guarantee our safety, because a social contract exists whereby the governed have granted the monarch absolute power over everyone. Hobbes's theory was not tied to any particular form of power, and he was logically able to return to England after the Civil Wars and accept the authority of Oliver Cromwell because it provided the guarantees needed to prevent a return to that state of nature in which life is 'solitary, poor, nasty, brutish and short'. Hobbes's ideas were regarded with great suspicion after the Restoration, especially since he accepted the principle that might is right and that a man who gains power by force of arms may be entrusted with supreme power as long as he can sustain it. This approach made no distinction between arbitrary or *de facto* sovereignty and legitimate (*de jure*) monarchy. Dryden was as much against absolute power as he was against usurpation of power by force, and objected to Hobbes in clear-cut terms:

> For who can be secure of private Right,
> If Sovereign sway may be dissolv'd by might? (779–80)

Cromwell's usurpation of royal power was a classic case of such arbitrariness. The royalist Samuel Butler complained ironically: 'The Hobbists will ... secure the Rights of Princes by asserting that whosoever can get their Power from them has right enough to it.' In Dryden's view, Hobbes's state of nature will return if we allow democratic power to prevail: not only kings but government itself will 'fall/To Natures state; where all have Right to all.' (793–4)

The Contexts of Absalom and Achitophel

Filmer

Much closer to Dryden's conservative position was Sir Robert Filmer's *Patriarcha: A Defence of the Natural Power of Kings*, written between 1635 and 1642 but published in 1680. He, too, abandons the older sacramental view of kingship, but rejects the newfangled materialist approach. Instead, he adopts a 'natural' interpretation of kingship, based upon the role of the father in the primitive family. In the Bible and in most known societies, he argued, power resides in the patriarch or father. By analogy, the king is the father of his people. Just as a patriarch's commands are arbitrary and are obeyed unquestioningly, so a king's must be accepted without question; otherwise there will be anarchy.

Locke

It was John Locke's theories of government which proved the most influential and representative of the new social and economic tendencies in Restoration England. He rejected Filmer's paternal model; we are not like the king's children. He proposed a fundamental distinction between our public and our private selves. In private we are separate and autonomous individuals, while in public we relate to one another in a legal sense, but even then we remain individuals and have a right to the ownership of the fruits of our labours. The major function of government, in his view, is to ensure the free possession and disposal of our private lives and property. Locke also rejected Hobbes's idea that in order to avoid a state of nature we require the overarching power of an absolute monarch. Because men are rational beings, they accept the law of nature as a *peaceful* law. We abandon a state of nature because scarcity requires it. However, civil government is limited and temperate, and governed by reason. Therefore, the monarchy should be limited and not absolute. While Dryden did not support an absolute monarchy either, he clearly did not see things in this way. Locke's views were those of the Whigs and the rising middle classes, who saw the opportunity of establishing a property-owning society, free from interference from court or church. The Civil Wars had been fought precisely over these questions. Ironically, Parliament had its way despite the Restoration.

Masterstudies: Absalom and Achitophel

'Democratic' ideas

During and immediately after the Civil Wars, with the lifting of censorship, there was a huge outpouring of radical political pamphlets. The most brilliant were those written by the Levellers, whose revolutionary doctrines were circulated through the New Model Army, Cromwell's great fighting force. They developed a very modern-sounding theory of government based upon the natural rights of the people. They proposed religious toleration, manhood suffrage (not for women or servants), universal education, no kings or lords, annual parliaments and a written constitution. Democracy in the United States was founded on very similar principles. However, in the 1640s these ideas seemed dangerous. John Lilburne was the best known of the Levellers. Gerard Winstanley, leader of the Diggers, combined radical politics, similar to the Levellers', with a mystical Protestant fervour. Samuel Butler, in *Hudibras*, published soon after the Restoration, took great pleasure in mocking such 'extremists', and Dryden, too, repeated the usual charges:

> A numerous Host of dreaming Saints succeed;
> Of the true old Enthusiastick breed:
> 'Gainst Form and Order they their Power employ;
> Nothing to Build and all things to Destroy. (529–32)

Most of the major figures of Augustan literature (even Swift) were politically conservative. Like Dryden, they all used the mockery of nonconformist religion and politics as a key weapon in their satiric writings.

Religion

Just as economic monopolies were challenged in the early part of the century, so too was the Church of England's monopoly on preaching. Being the state church, its interests were inextricably bound up with the crown's. The dignitaries of the church had great patronage which meant, inevitably, that their appointees tended to be conservative in outlook. However, during Elizabeth's reign efforts to suppress 'prophesyings' did not prevent the spread of lay-preaching. During the Civil Wars men began to demand that their preachers should be elected by their congregations. The revolutionary implications of this threat to the state church can be understood from the epigram which King James I is said to have uttered: 'No Bishop, no King, no nobility.'

The church courts, especially Archbishop Laud's Court of High Commission, were very powerful and could be convened on the demand of the monarch. Great friction between Charles I and Parliament was caused during the 1630s by the King's excessive use of the courts to raise money and to discipline the refractory. Such abuses were of long standing (Chaucer's Summoner complains likewise about the archdeacon's court). Many otherwise moderate men objected strongly to the Church's involvement in secular matters. It was not only Puritans and the merchant classes who objected, but also some of the gentry and the lawyers. The latter were an especially important weapon on Parliament's side, since they were able to argue that many of the powers of the Church courts should be exercised by the common-law courts, and in this they were appealing to ancient tradition.

Puritanism

James I's anxieties about the threat of Puritanism proved justified. During the 1640s they abolished the bishops, the House of Lords and the monarchy. 'Puritanism' is a broad term which includes several tendencies both inside and outside the state church. The Presbyterians were strong at the University of Cambridge and rejected episcopacy for a democratic system of church government involving elders and ministers on an equal footing. Puritans had high standards of integrity, a strong work ethic and a belief in the importance of the individual conscience. Luther's famous declaration 'Here I stand, so help me God, I can no other,' sums up this individualism. Puritans believed that men would be saved by their faith; good deeds should be expected of them, but they were not enough without faith. They emphasized preaching and intellectual conviction, and they regarded Catholics as too passive and devoted to empty ritual. The word 'zeal' was used by them and their enemies to describe their energetic faith. These attitudes explain their hostility to church decoration during the Civil Wars. With no radio, television, or newspapers (the latter were soon to arrive), preaching was an important channel not only of religious doctrine but of social and political thought. Puritans regarded the Anglican Church as 'popish'; its emphasis on prayer, ritual and ceremony was strongly encouraged by Archbishop Laud during the pre-revolutionary period. The Puritans felt that there was a need to revive the values expressed by Luther and Calvin in the Reformation. Their stress on the duty of hard work in one's calling made an important contribution to the rise of capitalism (see R. H. Tawney's famous *Religion and the Rise of Capitalism*). For the Puritan the whole of human life must be subordinated to God's purpose; there is no aspect of life which can be called secular. Dryden mocks this work ethic: ' 'tis Sin to misimploy an hour' (613). Puritans objected to the Bishops' encouragement of Sunday sports; the Sabbath was a day for preaching and discussion, not frivolity. The present-day struggle against 'Sunday opening' is a legacy of the sabbatism of our ancestors. Dryden ridicules Shimei's typically Puritan attitude to the Sabbath:

> [He] Did wisely from Expensive Sins refrain,
> And never broke the Sabbath, but for Gain: (587–8)

On the economic front Puritans favoured the confiscation of church property and revenues in order to finance a preaching ministry in every parish (many were without qualified ministers). With the help of merchants and lawyers they were able to finance the installation of a considerable number of Puritan preachers, but Laud suppressed the scheme. Another development was the growth of 'Independency'; congregations went above the heads of their bishops by selecting and financing ministers of their own choice. Laud's attempts to buy out church revenues which had been diverted to laymen offended many landowners and drove them into the arms of the Puritans.

At the start of the Civil Wars, Parliament instructed Puritan ministers to preach 'the truth and justice of Parliament's cause in taking up of defensive arms'. The state church was abolished and unacceptable ministers replaced by Puritans. The leading religious denominations on the 'Puritan' side were the Presbyterians, Independents, and Baptists. Presbyterians believed in a strong church government, and advocated a negotiated compromise with Charles I and the imposition of a strong ecclesiastical discipline. After the Restoration many Presbyterians preferred to go over to the Anglican Church rather than be forced into disabled Nonconformity. The Independents favoured the independence of each individual congregation (they influenced the later Congregationalists), argued a stronger line against the king, and promoted complete religious toleration. Their influence was paramount in the Roundheads' New Model Army. They were responsible for the regicide, which the Presbyterians never approved. Indeed the second Civil War saw the Scottish Presbyterians accept an 'Engagement' with the king to invade England, in return for the establishment of Presbyterianism in Scotland. The New Model Army proved victorious. During the wars there was some degree of toleration, which helped to keep the various, smaller religious sects committed to the Parliamentary cause. The sects' emphasis on equality appealed to the urban lower-middle class and the poor. Apart from the relatively sober Baptists, there were the more extreme groups, such as the Ranters, the Muggletonians, the Seekers and the Quakers. The Fifth

The Contexts of Absalom and Achitophel

Monarchists believed that Christ's second coming was imminent and advocated resistance to all government. Cromwell had to put down all such agitation. During this period most Puritans believed that God intended the betterment of man's life on earth. This was essentially a revolutionary view. The ultimate failure of the revolution led many of them to revise their attitude and argue that Christ's kingdom was, after all, not of this world.

Restoration Settlement

With the Restoration of the monarchy the Anglican Church was also restored, but never again held the position of political dominance it had with Laud. However, the old royalist Anglicans succeeded in excluding many, especially the Presbyterians, from the national church. Some blamed the failure of the scheme to establish a 'comprehensive' church on the Presbyterian Richard Baxter whose verbosity at the decisive Savoy Conference offended many. The intolerance of the newly established ruling-classes and attempts by Anglican clergy to impose uniformity upon their flocks were no less damaging to the cause of comprehensiveness. The second year of the Restoration saw the triumph of high Anglicanism and the exclusion of all the nonconforming clergy (the Act of Uniformity 1662).

The period 1660–1681 can be divided into three for our purposes:

(1) Between 1660 and 1672 the Dissenters were regarded as the most serious threat. Events such as Venner's rebellion in 1661 and his attempt to set up the reign of Christ on earth (the Fifth Monarchy) roused fears of new civil wars. Parliament saw to it that Nonconformists were excluded by law from public office. This was very much against the spirit of the Declaration of Breda in which Charles had written: 'We do declare a liberty to tender consciences'. However, in practice Nonconformists were often able to evade the law by 'occasional conformity' (occasionally taking the sacrament according to the Anglican rite, merely to qualify for public office). Those not prepared to compromise were often fined or imprisoned for worshipping in their own way, but occasionally were able to emerge from hiding, for example after the Declarations of Indulgence of 1662 and 1672.

(2) With the Declaration of 1672, the Test Act of 1673, and the disclosures of James's Catholicism, the fear of Roman Catholicism eclipsed fear of Dissent. There was some drawing together of Anglicans and

Masterstudies: Absalom and Achitophel

Dissenters against the common foe. The climax of this phase was, of course, the Popish Terror (1678–79).

(3) With the realization that the fear of Catholicism was being used by the Whigs in order to urge exclusion of James, the tide began to turn against the Dissenters once more during the great Tory reaction of 1681–5.

Finally, after the exile of James II in 1688, Parliament bowed to the inevitable and passed the Toleration Act, which allowed Dissenters freedom of worship.

In 1681 Dryden's attitude toward the Puritans, who had been much persecuted after 1660, is evident in the following passage on the London rabble ('The *Solymæan* rout'), who supported Shaftesbury (Achitophel), and were 'well Verst of old,/In Godly Faction':

> Hot *Levites* [Presbyterians] Headed these ...
> Resum'd their Cant, and with a Zealous Cry,
> Pursu'd their old belov'd Theocracy ...
> These led the Pack; tho not of surest scent,
> Yet deepest mouth'd against the Government.
> A numerous Host of dreaming Saints succeed;
> Of the true old Enthusiastick breed:
> 'Gainst Form and Order they their Power employ;
> Nothing to Build and all things to Destroy. (519, 521–2, 527–32)

Dryden retains a traditional anti-Puritan contempt which goes back especially to Ben Jonson's satiric comedies. 'Cant', 'Zeal', 'Enthusiastick' were the stock terms for Puritan language and religious feeling. Jonson's Ananias and Tribulation Wholesome refer to themselves as 'saints' and talk of their holy 'zeal' in *The Alchemist* (1610). The whole neo-classical literary tradition from Jonson through the Caroline poets to Dryden and Pope continued to mock the Puritans as hypocritical, vulgar and troublesome.

Whigs and Tories

The last ten years of Charles II's reign (1675–85) were some of the most complex and formative in the political history of Britain. During this period the two great political parties, the Whigs and the Tories, were formed. Danby, Charles's chief minister (1673–77), was the first party 'manager', who welded together the court party (later 'Tory') from the Cavalier supporters of the crown and the loyal members of the judiciary

The Contexts of Absalom and Achitophel

and church (the classic account is Keith Feiling's *History of the Tory Party 1640–1714*). Shaftesbury (Achitophel) shaped the Country party (later 'Whig') from those interest groups outside the court and Cavalier Parliament who wished to limit the power of the monarchy. He formed the Green Ribbon Club in Chancery Lane, where he organized a propaganda campaign against the court throughout the country. The campaign of petitions calling upon the king to meet Parliament was technically the beginning of the new party. The 'Petitioners' became the Whigs, and those who opposed the petitioning (the 'Abhorrers') became the Tories. The 'Whigs' drew their strength from the old Roundhead opposition to absolute monarchy and the fear of Catholicism.

The antagonisms between the court and country parties had deep roots in the old hostilities and fears which fermented the Civil Wars and were all too easily revived. The new nicknames repeat the old insults. The word 'Whig' is derived from the Scots word 'Whiggamore', an outlaw, especially one outlawed for political and religious opinion. 'Tory' is an Irish term for an outlaw and robber. The Scots were a thorn in the side of the monarchy before and during the Civil Wars; the 'Covenanters' fiercely resisted Charles I's attempt to impose episcopacy on Scotland. On the other side, the Roundheads always feared Ireland as a bastion of Catholicism, and Cromwell believed he was doing 'God's work' when he ruthlessly subjugated the island in 1650.

The enmities which are expressed in Dryden's *Absalom* were carried over from the Civil War. This can be clearly seen in Hobbes's famous Cavalier account of the Great Rebellion, as some prefer to call it. The following passage from his *Behemoth* (1667) gives the court party's view:

But the people were corrupted generally, and disobedient persons esteemed the best patriots ... the King's treasury was very low, and his enemies, that pretended the people's ease from taxes, and other specious things, had the command of the purses of the city of London ... The seducers were of divers sorts. One sort were ministers ... of Christ ['Presbyterians'] ... pretending to have a right from God to govern every one his parish, and their assembly the whole nation. Secondly, there were ... Papists.

Thirdly, there were not a few, who ... declared themselves for a liberty in religion ['Independents', 'Baptists', 'Fifth-monarchy-men', 'Quakers, Adamites, etc.'] ... And these were the enemies which arose against his Majesty from the private interpretation of the Scripture ...

Fourthly, there were an exceeding great number of men of the better sort [who were influenced by republican books in which] popular government was extolled by that glorious name of liberty ... they became thereby in love with their forms of government ...

Masterstudies: Absalom and Achitophel

Fifthly, the city of London and other great towns of trade, having in admiration the prosperity of the Low Countries after they had revolted from their monarch, the King of Spain, were inclined to think that the like change of government here, would to them produce the like prosperity.

Lastly, the people in general were so ignorant of their duty [to the King that they thought him] wisest and fittest to be chosen for a Parliament, that was most averse to the granting of subsidies or other public payments.

The malcontents mentioned here are precisely those described by Dryden in *Absalom*. It is as though the Civil Wars had never ended. The grievances of the Whigs were almost identical with their restive forebears. The following groups emerge clearly in Hobbes's analysis:
(1) The merchants of the City of London and other centres of trade
(2) The Republicans
(3) The Presbyterians, Independents and sectaries
(4) The gentry, represented by Parliament

While this does not provide an adequate analysis of the anti-royalist opposition from the point of view of modern historical scholarship, it reflects very faithfully the perceptions of the Tory faithful during the period of the Popish Plot and Exclusion Crisis. Hobbes conveniently overlooks the fact that the Whigs included a considerable proportion of landed nobility and gentry, as was the case too during the Civil Wars. Dryden does acknowledge that the opposition included peers but he dismisses them as 'mere Nobles' (see p. 47).

The Tories were no less subject to caricature than the Whigs. Here is a typical Whig description of a Tory:

A Tory is a monster with an English face, a French heart and an Irish conscience ... They are a sort of wild boars, that would root out the constitution ... that with dark lanthorn policies would at once blow up the two bulwarks of our freedom, Parliaments and Juries ... They are so certain that monarchy is *jure divino*, that they look upon all people living under Aristocracys or Democracys to be in a state of damnation.

From this and the Hobbes passage we can see how Dryden's poem takes up the typical idiom of the political parties of the time. Today we might hear socialists condemned as lackeys of the Soviets and conservatives mocked as agents of capitalism. In 1681, the Whigs accused the Tories of favouring Catholicism and Absolutism and trying to undermine 'freedom', parliaments and juries. The Tories accused the Whigs of religious fanaticism, economic selfishness, false patriotism and republicanism. The Tories continually dragged in the old Civil War smears. The Whigs were 'Scottish Covenanters', 'Geneva Doctors' (Calvin lived in Geneva), and 'Presbyterians'. All these claims and counterclaims are represented in the witty satire of *Absalom*.

The Whig view, which was temporarily eclipsed during James II's reign (1685–88), was ultimately victorious, because it represented causes and attitudes which were in harmony with the general social and economic development of Britain and also 'progressive' on questions of personal liberty. Ogg's summary of their distinctive doctrines is as follows:

> that the judicial bench should be independent of the court; that the military forces should be parliamentary; that ministerial responsibility should be enforced by an unrestrained right to use the weapon of impeachment; that Parliament should have the right to debate and criticize the king's speeches; and that placemen should be excluded from the House of Commons.

It would be wrong to deduce from all this abuse and caricature that the two budding political parties and the interests they represented were bent upon undoing one another and starting a new civil war. It is important to note that the Whigs were not on the whole republican in sympathy: they favoured a constitutional monarchy, a compromise which suited their commitment to freedom in trade and religion. The Tories on the whole did not favour a monarchy modelled on the absolutism of Louis XIV. They were mainly committed to the Anglican Church and shared some of the Whig distaste for continental Catholicism. However, though at first they were swept along with the nationalist Protestant passion against the Catholics during the early days of the Popish Terror, they regained their balance by 1680 and began to resist the Whig party-line. Despite the language of Dryden's poem, there was on the whole an avoidance of extremism on both sides, which we have come to regard as typically English. On the other hand, one should not underestimate the seriousness of the Exclusion Crisis; it certainly must have *seemed* to a loyalist like Dryden that the 'Good old Cause' was once again rearing its ugly head.

Literature and Science

It is usual to refer to the dominant literary culture between 1660 and 1780 as 'Augustan' or 'neo-classical'. Both terms refer to the importance of Roman literature and history for the period. During the later seventeenth century, the beginnings of journalism and the rise of middle-class culture started to produce a new professional group of writers, who were ridiculed and insulted by the 'Augustans'. However, most writers still relied, for support and advancement, on patrons to whom they dedicated

Masterstudies: Absalom and Achitophel

their writings. The major figures, such as Dryden, Swift and Pope, liked to compare themselves with the great poets of the Augustan period in Rome – Virgil, Horace and Ovid, who were also patronized by the great men of state including the emperor Augustus. Dryden translated Virgil's *Æneid* (1697) and Swift and Pope wrote imitations of Horace. Not only did they absorb the classics directly, but they adopted the stylistic values of the Augustans. Pope and Swift often expressed their disgust with the Whig Prime Minister, Sir Robert Walpole ('Bob the poet's foe'), who, in their view, patronized the hacks and not the good authors.

Augustan Aesthetics

I shall call the literary ideas of the early Augustans an 'aesthetic ideology', because their social, religious, political and moral ideas were inextricably linked with their aesthetic ideas. To put it another way, their aesthetics corresponded to their general ideology. The end of the Civil Wars and Commonwealth, like the end of the civil wars of the Roman Republic, released them, they believed, from a long, dark night of brutality, vulgarity and obscurity. During the Royalist exile in France refinement and sophistication were acquired not only by the royalist poets but also by the court, which returned in 1660 with new standards of 'conversation' and style. Despite these developments, Shakespeare and Ben Jonson were still regarded as great writers. Dryden's admiration of both was eloquently expressed in his criticism. However, many Restoration writers believed that the Elizabethan poets lived in ignorant times. Dryden said of Shakespeare that, although he was a great *natural* poet, he lacked refinement. Dr Johnson believed that it was Dryden who finally brought English poetry into the light; he 'refined the language, improved the sentiments, and tuned the numbers [versification] of English poetry'. Dryden's immediate predecessors, Cowley, Waller and Denham, were often celebrated as refiners of poetry, although their reputations did not remain high after the eighteenth century.

Dryden regarded Sir John Denham's poem *Cooper's Hill* (1642) as a model of literary expression: it had 'the majesty of style' which is 'the exact standard of good writing'. His lines on the river Thames have often been cited as a perfect embodiment of Augustan aesthetics:

> O could I flow like thee, and make thy stream
> My great example, as it is my theme!
> Though deep, yet clear, though gentle, yet not dull,
> Strong without rage, without ore-flowing full.

The Contexts of Absalom and Achitophel

Notice the subtle balance of phrase against phrase, the studied moderation of attitude (the poem was written at the start of the Civil Wars) and the elegant rhythm.

'Dignity', 'majesty', 'correctness', 'ease', 'clarity' and 'polish'. These were the standard epithets used to describe good verses. It is not without significance that they might also be used to convey the manners of a courtier. Such a standard was socially exclusive and encouraged the mockery of those who fell below it or simply stood outside it. The ridicule and assured poise to be found in *Absalom and Achitophel* were made possible by this cultured tradition. All writing, past and present, was subjected to this standard of excellence. The metaphysical poets, for example, were considered barbarous in their obscurity and pedantry. Poetry should not be too clever, but should aim to say things with elegant clarity. Donne's use of conceits (far-fetched metaphors) and puns were considered poor taste and unnatural. Dryden admired Donne's intellectual power, but thought him too subtle and unmusical. He himself wrote in the metaphysical manner in his early poetry (for example his rather grotesque elegy 'Upon the Death of Lord Hastings', written while still at Westminster school) but had it out of his system by the end of the 1660s.

Science and Language

The Augustan insistence on clarity of expression was connected with scientific and philosophical developments during the century. Francis Bacon was the father of the scientific revolution and he fought hard to overcome the traditional obstacles to scientific advancement; among these he paid special attention to the abuse of words. All the loving care which writers had lavished on their style suddenly appeared to be a foolish indulgence because it tended to obscure the simple statement of a fact or the clear perception of a thing. Nature now seemed to require the suppression of unnecessary words, in order to allow the objects of nature to impress themselves directly upon the human mind. Both the complicated intellectual systems of medieval philosophy and the elaborate eloquence of fashionable 'Ciceronian' prose made it more difficult to fit words to things, for 'words are but the images of matter'. Bacon's programme for the advancement of science inspired the founding of the Royal Society in 1662. One of its early steps was to set up 'a committee for improving the English language'. One of its members was John Dryden. Thomas Sprat, the historian of the Society, expressed the stylistic ideals which were to be advanced: it was necessary to avoid 'swellings of style', 'to return back to the primitive purity, and shortness, when men delivered so many *things* almost in an equal number of *words*', and to bring 'all things as near the mathematical plainness as they can'.

Obviously, these were requirements for scientific discourse, not for literature, but they still influenced attitudes to expression. Augustan writers frequently praised the virtues of simplicity and clarity which they found in classical literature, and which were being given high status by the modern scientific community. We now consider that such an ideal of language is not only arid but unrealistic. Modern philosophy and linguistics have abandoned the naive view of language, which likens it to a mirror capable of reflecting things. Language has an independent reality too. Dryden was perfectly aware of this when he said, of metre and rhythm, that 'versification and numbers are the greatest pleasures of poetry'. While, like all good Augustans, he acknowledged that poetry should 'instruct', he often placed an emphasis on pleasure: 'Poetry instructs only as it delights.' In the preface to *Absalom* he suggests that aesthetic pleasure can over-rule intellectual objections: 'For there's a sweetness in good Verse, which Tickles even while it hurts: And, no man can be heartily angry with him, who pleases him against his will.' However, neither instruction nor pleasure can be said to have much to do with reflecting things directly in words. When Dryden actually discusses the problem of imitating nature he concludes, in *A Defence of an Essay of Dramatic Poesy*, that ' 'Tis true that to imitate well is a poet's work; but to affect the soul, and excite the passions, and above, all, to move admiration, . . . a bare imitation will not serve.' Indeed, what a poet imitates 'must be heightened with all the arts and ornaments of poesy'. One may conclude that poets paid lip-service to the ideals of modern science, but that they also silently upheld the different ideals of poetic expression.

DESCARTES

It is worth adding that the French philosopher, René Descartes, perhaps best expressed the ideals of Augustan aesthetics. He believed that philosophy needed a new method which resembled mathematics or, more specifically, geometry; it aimed at certainty by trying to achieve *clear and distinct* ideas of things: 'all things which we very clearly and distinctly conceive are true'. We should try to understand things in their simplest and even most abstract form. Following these ideals, Augustan poetry avoids inessential detail and tries to give us the purest and most general apprehension of a thing or event or person. Dr Johnson later referred to this when he wrote: 'all great truths are general.' This explains why Augustan poetry is more abstract, less personal, and less 'realistic' than Romantic or modern literature.

4 Satire

Conventions used in Dryden's Absalom

Dryden is inventive in the way he puts together certain traditional forms. It may help the reader to survey briefly the main conventions which he builds into his satiric structure.

(1) Character sketches are one of the prominent features of *Absalom*. Personal portraits, whether satiric or eulogistic, are interspersed throughout the narration. Not only was there a lively seventeenth-century vogue for the Theophrastan 'character', but the best Elizabethan and Restoration dramatists favoured the use of studied character sketches in order to give vitality to individual roles. Ben Jonson, in scholarly fashion, drew upon the classical historians for his characterizations (for example in his use of Tacitus in *Sejanus*). Restoration historians too were expert in drawing such sketches (especially Clarendon in his *History of the Great Rebellion* and Gilbert Burnet in his *Life of My Own Time*).

(2) Set speeches are used in *Absalom* to expose the folly or wickedness of a character. The great advantage of this was that characters are made to damn themselves rather than be subjected to direct abuse or detraction. Drama and epic were the main models for this device. Dryden was especially indebted, it seems, to Milton's wonderful set speeches in the underworld scenes of *Paradise Lost*, Books I and II.

(3) This is combined in Milton and Dryden with the epic 'catalogue of forces'. Both writers include impressive catalogues of enemy forces (the wise counsellors in *Absalom* are a secondary and shorter list).

Dryden's Rejection of Rough Satire

During the period following the restoration of the monarchy (1660), neo-classical poets such as Dryden recognized the greatness of Elizabethan and Jacobean literature, but also believed that the advances in refinement since 1600 limited its value as a literary model. Even Shakespeare was regarded as being primitive in certain respects (see also p. 82). Dryden considered the Elizabethans to have had more genius but less skill. Elizabethan verse satirists such as John Donne, Joseph Hall and John Marston wrote in a consciously rough and obscure way, in the belief that this was the appropriate style for satire. This view of the genre persisted even into the Restoration period itself, for example in the satires of John Oldham and Thomas Shadwell. The latter wrote: 'I do not think great smoothness is required in a *Satyr*, which ought to have a *severe* kind of *roughness* as most fit for *reprehension*'. Fortunately for our account, Dryden wrote one of his best poems in memory of Oldham, who died young in 1683. Even though Dryden had to preserve the generosity of spirit appropriate to an elegy, he manages to handle an important criticism of Oldham's satires with some delicacy:

> O early ripe! to thy abundant store
> What could advancing Age have added more?
> It might (what Nature never gives the young)
> Have taught the numbers [i.e. metrical smoothness] of thy native Tongue.
> But Satyr needs not those, and Wit will shine
> Through the harsh cadence of a rugged line.

Dryden tactfully protects Oldham from the full force of the criticism he makes of his rough verses by conceding that 'Satyr needs not those'. However, we know from Dryden's own theory and practice that he did not really believe this. His own great satires are as elegantly and smoothly written as an epic poem.

Satire and the Heroic

Before examining Dryden's own theory of satire more closely, it is necessary to discuss the satiric uses of heroic or epic poetry in this period. Ever since the Romans, satirists had indulged in parody of epic poetry. In the seventeenth century the French satirist Scarron wrote 'travesties' of classical epic which retold the originals in vulgar style. Here is a passage from Charles Cotton's *Virgile Travestie* on Æneas, the hero of Virgil's *Æneid*:

> I sing the man (read it who list,
> A Trojan true as ever pissed)
> Who from Troy town, by wind and weather,
> To Italy (and God knows whither)
> Was packed, and wracked, and lost, and tossed,
> And bounced from pillar unto post.

The most famous early Restoration satirist was Samuel Butler who, in *Hudibras*, burlesqued heroic writings, using both a low style *and* a low subject matter (the story of an itinerant Presbyterian and his sectarian squire). In his *Mac Flecknoe* Dryden perfected the mock-heroic satire, in which a low subject (the feeble poet Shadwell) is ridiculed by the epic style. Finally, in *Absalom and Achitophel*, he wrote what we must call heroic satire, in which a predominantly high style is combined with a high subject matter – important affairs of state. We may summarize the different kinds of satire we have described:

(1) *Travesty*: parody of a particular heroic poem, using a low style. Example: James Scudamore's *Homer à la Mode* (1664).

(2) *Burlesque*: a general parody of the heroic, using a low style *and* a low subject in a heroic guise. Example: Butler's *Hudibras* (1663, 1664, 1678).

(3) *Mock-heroic*: a parody of the heroic, using a high style and a low subject. Example: Dryden's *Mac Flecknoe* (1684).

(4) *Heroic Satire*: a general parody of the heroic, using a high style and a high subject. Example: Dryden's *Absalom and Achitophel* (1681).

One must say immediately that this is only a generalized scheme. In *Absalom*, for example, although the subject matter is of great moment and the main protagonists are leading figures of state, not all the characters in the poem are 'high'. The portrait of Corah, for example, has more in common with the mock-heroic treatment of Shadwell in *Mac Flecknoe*.

Marvell and Oldham

Dryden's immediate precursors in 'heroic' satire were Andrew Marvell and John Oldham. Marvell, MP for Hull, whose pre-Restoration poetry had been predominantly lyric, began to write satires on behalf of the country party in opposition to the court. He was upholding the tradition of Parliamentary opposition to the monarch's absolutist leanings. He seized upon the royalist panegyrics of the 1660s which were written in the first flush of the new reign. Their celebration of the new regime was often grotesquely exaggerated and inflated; at least, this was how they appeared to many sceptical readers. Edmund Waller's celebration of James's victory over the Dutch at Lowestoft in June 1665 uses an Italian poetic device of having the poet instruct a painter on the heroic scene to be painted. *Instructions to a Painter* contains a number of features common to the heroic style of Restoration panegyrics (see p. 91) and heroic plays. These presented the satirist with a perfect opportunity for ridicule, especially since this poem and other panegyrics of the same type were overinflated and without real grandeur. Marvell's satiric *The Last Instructions to a Painter* (1667) is the most impressive of a long series of 'Painter' poems by him and others. It anticipates Dryden in being a

Masterstudies: Absalom and Achitophel

comprehensive treatment of public affairs. Unlike *Absalom* its form is not related to epic; it is a chronicle history without any strongly organized poetic form. The poem includes inset portraits of individuals (see above) and also panegyrics (like Dryden's on Ossory). Also, like Dryden's poem, it deals with an immediate national crisis. However, the Parliamentary conflicts arising from the Dutch Wars are treated from the point of view of the Country (later Whig) Party. Among the wide variety of styles employed in the poem by Marvell are some which anticipate Dryden: he combines urbane 'raillery' (see below) and majestic invective; and he uses the weighty and dignified heroic style of Virgil for satiric purposes. A striking example is his description of Charles, who while musing 'on th' uneasy throne', has a nocturnal vision in the manner of Macbeth or Richard III:

> Paint last the King and a dead shade of night,
> Only dispers'd by a weak taper's light . . .
> There, as in th' calm horror all alone
> He wakes and muses of th' uneasy throne,
> Raise up a sudden shape with virgin's face.

So far this is in pure heroic style. Marvell brilliantly modulates into satire in his account of the king's characteristically amorous response to the vision:

> The object strange in him no terror mov'd:
> He wonder'd first, then piti'd, then he lov'd
> And with kind hand does the coy vision press
> (Whose beauty greater seem'd by her distress),
> But soon shrunk back, chill'd with her touch so cold,
> And th' airy picture vanish'd from his hold.

Marvell shows great skill in combining an echo of Virgil's *Æneid* (in Book VI Dido's ghost appears to Æneas in the underworld) with a satiric account of Charles's sexual disappointment.

John Oldham's *Satyrs upon the Jesuits* (1681) uses the more exaggerated style of the heroic plays for his violent Juvenalian satires against the Jesuits, written during the early stages of the Terror which followed the allegations of Titus Oates. Dryden's training in the use of heroic style was completed during the 1660s and 1670s when he wrote a number of 'heroic' plays. Grandiose heroes, eastern potentates and passionate lovers strut upon the stage, proclaiming their ambitions and giving vent to their passions in long bombastic speeches. Here is a passage from Torrismond's speech in Dryden's *The Spanish Fryar* (produced *c.* spring 1681):

> Good Heav'ns, why gave you me a Monarch's Soul,
> And crusted it with base Plebeian Clay!
> Why gave you me Desires of such extent,
> And such a Span to grasp 'em? Sure my Lot
> By some o'er-hasty Angel was misplac'd
> In Fate's eternal Volume!

The alert reader will notice the similarity of these lines to those put into Absalom's mouth when he laments his 'mean Descent' (366). The contemporary reader would have enjoyed the parody of heroic style and seen Absalom's speech as an absurdly posturing one.

Virgil and Horace

Dryden was also a master of the authentic heroic style of the Roman poet Virgil, whose *Æneid* he translated towards the end of his life. Virgil was a model of elegance, majesty, dignity and good sense. The use of Virgilian epic style in satire counterbalanced the more exaggerated expression of the heroic drama. Oldham did not temper his satires in this way, but gave full rein to bombastic ranting in the manner of the heroic drama. In *Absalom* Dryden achieved a further delicacy by combining his heroic mode with Horatian 'fine raillery' (see below on Dryden's *Discourse*). In the preface 'To the Reader' he hopes to 'please the more Moderate sort', and has therefore aimed at 'rebating the *Satyre*, (where Justice would allow it) from carrying too sharp an Edge'. He goes on to write in terms which are evidently Horatian: 'I have but laught at some mens Follies, when I coud have declaim'd against their Vices'. We discuss the political significance of Dryden's stance of moderation elsewhere (see p. 24). The softening of the edge of satire in 'fine raillery' is balanced by important passages of genuine epic grandeur, notably the last lines of *Absalom I* in which the monarch prevails:

> He said. Th' Almighty, nodding, gave Consent;
> And Peals of Thunder shook the Firmament.
> Henceforth a Series of new time began,
> The mighty Years in long Procession ran:
> Once more the Godlike *David* was Restor'd,
> And willing Nations knew their Lawfull Lord. (1026-31)

Not only is the subject sublime ('Godlike *David*', 'Lawfull Lord'), but there is a clear echo of Virgil's famous fourth eclogue, in which a new age dawns with the birth of the consul Pollio's son – a new age marked,

Masterstudies: Absalom and Achitophel

one should notice, by a *restoration*: *'Iam Redit et Virgo, Redeunt Saturnia Regna'* (Now returns the Maid [Justice], and the reign of Saturn returns). As George deForest Lord has pointed out, Dryden skilfully adopts a cyclical version of history which underlies his conservative vision of perpetual recurrence and restoration of truth and law.

Milton

Milton's *Paradise Lost* (1667) was the only great epic poem written in Dryden's period. It made an important contribution to the poem's effectiveness in damning Absalom and Achitophel and elevating David. In the preface Dryden lays the foundation of a profound analogy between the actions of the protagonists in his poem and those of Milton's epics (*Paradise Regained* is also used). He refers to Adam's temptations and Achitophel's satanic nature: " 'tis no more a wonder that he [Absalom] withstood not the temptations of *Achitophel*, than it was for *Adam*, not to have resisted the two Devils; the Serpent, and the Woman.' Dryden cleverly connects Achitophel with Satan while retaining his usual stance of moderation and good nature: 'I have not, so much as an uncharitable Wish against *Achitophel*; but, am content to be accus'd of a good natur'd Errour; and, to hope with *Origen* [one of the church fathers] that the Devil himself may, at last, be sav'd.' In the poem itself there is an underlying allusion to Satan's rebellion in *Paradise Lost*, both in the conspiracy against Charles and in the temptation of Monmouth by Shaftesbury. The temptation scenes are modelled initially on the temptation of Christ in *Paradise Regained*: Achitophel refers to Absalom's 'Nativity', and speaks of him as *'Saviour'* and 'Their second *Moses*'. We remember that Christ too was a son of David. There is another subtle linking of Absalom and Christ when we read of David's admiration for him:

> With secret Joy, indulgent *David* view'd
> His Youthfull Image in his Son renew'd. (31–2)

This not only alludes to Christ, 'the son of David', but also to God's love for his own son. Later, as Absalom weakens, Achitophel tempts him as Satan tempted Eve. Dryden cleverly prepares the ground for this in his opening description of Absalom's beauty: 'And *Paradise* was open'd in his face.' (30) Later, as Absalom weakens further, the parallel with Milton's poem is evident in the style:

Satire

> Him Staggering so when Hells dire Agent found,
> While fainting Vertue scarce Maintain'd her Ground,
> He pours fresh Forces in, and thus Replies: (373–5)

Notice the use of Miltonic inversion in the first line (for 'When Hells dire Agent found Him Staggering'). Achitophel himself, in his temptation of Absalom, compares Charles's precarious state with Satan's fall from heaven:

> But, like the Prince of Angels from his height,
> [He] Comes tumbling downward with diminish'd light; (273–4)

reminding us of Milton's description of the fallen angels in Book I of *Paradise Lost*. The parallel is, of course, ironic, coming from Achitophel, who is trying to tempt Absalom to rebel against godlike David.

Panegyric

The last section made it clear that Dryden's conception of satire was deeply influenced by heroic poetry. However, it was not only epic poetry and the heroic drama which provided his models. The formal panegyric was an important literary form in classical literature and in the seventeenth century. The Greek poet Pindar wrote panegyric odes celebrating the heroes of the Greek games and elevating them to the level of gods. The Roman tradition developed the political role of the panegyric. The form was used by Pliny the Younger and others to celebrate the institution of the empire, to announce the coming of a new age, and to offer instruction in the office of emperor. The Roman panegyrics often include a strongly oratorical element: they are written as if for public delivery or for a specific public occasion. From the beginning of the seventeenth century the term 'panegyric' was used by English poets for their poems addressed to the monarch. They were public celebrations of virtue, nobility and splendour. The extent to which they drew upon the various classical functions of panegyric varied, but by the time of Dryden the form had been fully exploited, especially by Edmund Waller in his panegyrics to Cromwell and Charles II and by Dryden himself in his poems addressed to Charles II.

The panegyrics, written for Charles's restoration, in and soon after 1660 were the last full flowering of the form. Unlike the panegyric epistles written by Cavalier poets for their beloved monarch, Restoration poets usually wrote such verses for hire. At best they were highly professional and polished poems for particular occasions or to celebrate important persons. At their worst they were mere hack work. Elkanah

Masterstudies: Absalom and Achitophel

Settle (Doeg in *Absalom II*) had such verses ready-written with blank spaces for the names to be filled in as appropriate! Attitudes to heroism, to monarchy and towards nobility and the divine underwent a radical change in the later seventeenth century, at least in the dominant polite society. Critics often talk, rather loosely but not entirely inaccurately, of the period 1660–1780 as the 'Age of Reason', referring to the shift away from ideologies which were fundamentally God-centred to those which rely heavily on common sense, immediate sense-experience, and an emphasis on natural causes. Gradually it no longer seemed sensible to believe in the supernatural. Hobbes's well-known rationalist arguments against medieval romances were typical of this new outlook:

> There are some that are not pleased with fiction, unless it be bold, not only to exceed the work, but also the possibility of nature: they would have impenetrable armours, enchanted castles. invulnerable bodies . . . flying horses, and a thousand such things . . . In old time amongst the heathens such strange fictions and metamorphoses were not so remote from the articles of their faith as they are now from ours.

Such scepticism seems a poor soil for the panegyric which so often indulges in extravagant praise and lofty themes. However, the Augustans permitted themselves some carefully controlled flights of enthusiasm which preserved good sense and reason.

Dryden's major panegyrics were *Astraea Redux* (1660) and *To His Sacred Majesty, A Panegyrick on His Coronation* (1661), both addressed to Charles. Dryden considered panegyric to be a branch of heroic poetry. His account of the hero in epic poetry is closely connected with the panegyric hero: 'The shining quality of an epic hero, his magnanimity, his constancy, his patience, his piety . . . raises first our admiration'. Dryden noticeably diverts attention away from the hero's military prowess towards his *moral* stature. A true monarch combines the qualities of the Virgilian hero (Æneas was 'pius') and the Christian hero. Charles is Augustus and Christ rolled into one. Milton's view of heroism in *Paradise Lost* is similar: he rejects the martial heroism of Achilles for the 'heroic martyrdom' of Christ (in *Samson Agonistes* the hero's death in the temple brings together active *and* passive heroism). I have drawn attention to this aspect of the heroic and panegyric tradition, because it helps us to appreciate Dryden's emphasis on Charles's merciful and lenient image in *Absalom*.

Another aspect of Dryden's panegyrics which is relevant to the satires is their black and white view of politics. The forces of good and evil are lined up all too clearly. James Garrison sums up this feature as follows:

Satire

'The rigorous distinction between the two sources of power, between divine monarch and the infernal usurper, between love and force, between peace and war, is fundamental to the genre ... Traditional panegyric is a ceremonial confirmation of an institution that exists rightfully, lawfully and by divine will.' It is evident that all this is directly relevant to *Absalom*. Absalom and Achitophel and their supporters are the satanic rebels, while David is their 'Godlike' and 'Lawfull' lord. In *Astraea Redux* the Civil Wars are evoked and, as in *Absalom*, we are given lurid pictures of the fearful multitude:

> The rabble now such freedom did enjoy
> As winds at sea that use it to destroy:
> Blind as the Cyclops and as wild as he,
> They owned a lawless savage liberty.

Charles is King David and 'great Augustus'; he returns not to wreak vengeance but to offer Christ-like forgiveness. There is a historical basis for this claim: whatever vengeance had to be pursued was undertaken by Parliament, while Charles held firmly to his provisional amnesty in the Declaration of Breda. He has his father's 'mildness' and finds 'Revenge less sweet than a forgiving mind'. The poem concludes with a frequently borrowed theme from the underworld scene in Book VI of Virgil's *Æneid* in which the future glory of the Roman empire is announced, and the coming of the long foretold Augustus, 'Born to restore a better age of gold' (Dryden's translation). It will be both a restoration and a new age. Charles's restoration brings in a new era:

> And now Time's whiter series is begun,
> Which in soft centuries shall smoothly run.

Similarly, at the end of *Absalom* 'Godlike *David*' is 'Restor'd', and

> Henceforth a Series of new time began,
> The mighty Years in long Procession ran: (1028–9)

So far we have discussed the common themes of panegyric and heroic satire. However, Dryden not only uses the heroic genres in order to elevate his theme, but also invents an ironic use for panegyric in Achitophel's temptation of Absalom. Here, Achitophel, the panegyric orator, first praises Absalom ('Auspicious Prince! . . .', lines 230 ff.), and then offers his prince political advice (lines 244 ff.). So, Dryden embraces the values of heroic poetry and upholds the sovereignty of the monarch; and at the same time he gives us an inverted heroic orator, who uses the panegyric form to undermine a peaceful monarchy by recommending rebellion.

Masterstudies: Absalom and Achitophel

Dryden's Discourse

Dryden's *Discourse concerning the Original and Progress of Satire* (1693) is the chief critical discussion of verse satire in the Augustan period. Dryden examines in detail the characteristics of classical satirists, especially Horace and Juvenal. During the Renaissance most discussions of satire treated the two Roman satirists as representative of the two essential styles of satire. It was usual to regard Horace as a 'comic' satirist, and Juvenal as 'tragic'. Julius Caesar Scaliger preferred Juvenal's *maiestas* (grandeur) and declamatory power, while Heinsius and Vossius preferred the more prosaic and humorous Horace. These discussions influenced all subsequent ones. In the seventeenth century it was usual to indicate a preference one way or the other. A writer might declare his commitment to attacking vice, or his desire not to give offence to the great and to mock only people's follies. During Dryden's period, Horace and Juvenal were widely read, translated and imitated. The developing Augustan values of 'common sense', 'moderation', 'clarity' and 'naturalness' would appear to favour Horace. But, in fact, Juvenal was just as popular, if not more so.

In the *Discourse*, Dryden is attracted to Horace's undogmatic approach to life, and his 'good-natured' tone of voice, which treats men's failings with a tolerant humour. Horace refuses to write libels against individuals. Such venomous attacks are totally without wit and 'pleasantry'. We note that satire against an individual is justified only if 'he is become a public nuisance'. Dryden's attack on Monmouth and Shaftesbury are clearly justified on this criterion. However, he avoids the crude kinds of attack used in libel or lampoon, preferring to be more refined and witty. The biblical allegory and the ironic use of heroic style cushion the satire and give the reader the pleasure of subtlety and stylishness.

But Dryden does not find everything necessary for satire in Horace, who lacks the 'more vigorous and masculine Wit' of Juvenal. Juvenal expresses a more majestic indignation. Dryden believed that the French satirist Boileau achieved this perfection by introducing into his satires 'the majesty of the heroic', which is 'finely mixed with the venom' of satire. So, good nature is not enough; it would be insipid without the nobility and majesty of heroic verse. Juvenal's style is 'sonorous' and 'noble', in keeping with his 'sublime and lofty' thoughts. However, having apparently retracted his praise of Horace, Dryden declares 'I cannot give ... up the manner of Horace ... so easily', because, in the end, 'the nicest and most delicate touches of satires consist in fine raillery'. He cites his own characterization of Zimri in *Absalom* as an example of 'fine raillery', which avoids 'the mention of great crimes', and represents only 'blindsides, and little extravagances'. Dryden argues amusingly for a certain delicacy in satiric portraits:

How easy is it to call rogue and villain, and that wittily! But how hard to make a man appear a fool, a blockhead, or a knave, without using any of those opproprious terms! ... There is ... a vast difference betwixt the slovenly butchering of a man, and the fineness of a stroke that separates the head from the body, and leaves it standing in its place.

In the preface to *Absalom* he makes the similar point that the corrective purpose of satire should be achieved without resorting to 'the chirurgeon's [surgeon's] work of an *ense rescindendum* [something to be cut out with the sword]'. Dryden seems to believe that provided it is done with skill and panache, it is all right to behead a man metaphorically, since he will not feel it. One draws the conclusion that the ethical good sense of Horace is to be combined with the stylistic good sense of Juvenal, that the 'venom' of satire is to be tempered by the nobility of epic verse, that good manners require the savour of 'masculine wit' and noble 'spleen'.

His flexible theory of satire enabled Dryden to use a wide range of satiric tones from the heroic ridicule of Absalom and Achitophel through the delicate raillery of the Zimri portrait to the harsher and more scurrilous treatment of Shimei and Corah.

Lampoon

The lampoon or literary libel appeared as a literary form in England at the beginning of the seventeenth century, when over-clever students of the inns of court and other young literati wrote recondite, obscene and rugged satires against their enemies. Various terms – satire, libel, lampoon – were used indiscriminately during the Restoration period. As we have seen, Dryden carefully distinguishes between various types of satire, in order to distance himself from the cruder 'lampoon', which he regards as a lower form of satire, only justified in extreme cases. Vast numbers of topical or personal lampoons were written during this period, though not many have survived. They were chiefly attacks on ladies of dubious virtue, poets, politicians, kings or anyone who for any reason achieved some notoriety. The court wits and their associates were especially prolific in such writings. The Earls of Dorset and Mulgrave, the

Masterstudies: Absalom and Achitophel

Duke of Buckingham, Sir George Etherege, Sir Charles Sedley, Henry Killigrew and of course the Earl of Rochester were among the leading lampooners of the age. Sometimes an exchange of abuse between two exponents of the vogue has survived, for example that between Rochester and Sir Carr Scroope. The nearsighted Scroope recognized himself in Rochester's insulting phrase 'the Pur-blind Knight' and replied in 'In Defense of Satire', goading Rochester with a reference to his ignoble behaviour in deserting the fatally injured Captain Downes in 1676. The exchange continued. Rochester called Scroope 'a lump deformed', 'an Ugly Beau-Garcon'. Scroope replied by describing Rochester as 'full of Pox and Malice'.

Since Restoration politics generated so much passion and hatred, it is scarcely surprising that it also generated a goodly number of lampoons and libels. Some of the wits stood above politics and ridiculed both court and country, but many more were written for party purposes. Attribution of the poems is often uncertain, but we know that the Duke of Buckingham, one of the authors of *The Rehearsal*, which satirized Dryden, was the object of many attacks and wrote many libels himself. The Earl of Mulgrave, a leading Tory, devoted a part of his *Essay on Satire* (1679) to attacking Buckingham, Shaftesbury, Halifax and Heneage Finch, the Lord Chancellor, three of whom were also targets in the two parts of *Absalom*.

We have already mentioned that Dryden rejected the ethos of the lampoon. However, his portrait of Shadwell in *Mac Flecknoe* seems not to conform to his high-minded principles. The satire is personal and not matched by anything in Shadwell's prior references to Dryden or justified by Shadwell's public nuisance value, except insofar as bad poets are a public nuisance. The attack is concerned with Shadwell's *literary* shortcomings and is mitigated only by the distancing effect of the mock-heroic device; the heroic framework gives the satire an aesthetic impersonality which elevates it above mere libel. There is much less distancing of the attack in *Absalom* Part II, in which Settle and Shadwell are so mercilessly pilloried. The passage on Og is highly personal, both in its physical description and its tone. However, unlike the Shadwell of *Mac Flecknoe*, Og can be seen as a public nuisance: he rolls home from a '*Treason* Tavern', where he has presumably been contriving antigovernment pamphlets on behalf of the Whigs.

While it is evident that hard and fast distinctions between true satire and libel or lampoon tend to break down, Dryden's own practice conforms for the most part to his principles. He adjusts his tone and style according to the occasion and the purpose of his satire. Even in *Absalom*

Part II when he lampoons Settle and Shadwell, he manages to preserve the essential Augustan values of correctness and control, never descending to 'the slovenly butchering of a man'. The modern reader may feel that however well-sharpened the blade, it does the same damage, only more neatly. But, as any fencing expert would say, to score with style makes all the difference!

5 Biblical Allegory and Typology

Dryden's use of analogy or parallel between biblical history and contemporary history was not new, but his application is uniquely subtle and rich. Behind it lies a long history of medieval and renaissance interpretation of scripture. Traditions of exegesis varied, but all insisted that holy writ had more than just a single literal meaning. The most common division was between (1) literal, (2) moral and (3) allegorical interpretations. Dryden's view of the value of allegory can be understood from his discussion of history in the *Life of Plutarch* (1683): history 'helps us to judge of what will happen, by showing us the like revolutions of former times'. Since human nature is always the same, all we need is 'judgement enough to draw the parallel'. Absalom's and Achitophel's conspiracy against David is an archetypal story which tells us something about political history in all times and places. Dryden's judgement in drawing out the parallels for his time is unmatched in seventeenth-century writings.

The biblical history is taken from II Samuel 13–18. The following is a summary:

13: Amnon, son of David, forces his sister Tamar to lie with him. His brother Absalom takes revenge by arranging his death and then goes into voluntary exile. David has no desire to punish his beloved Absalom and laments his departure.

14: Absalom's beauty is described: 'from the sole of his foot even to the crown of his head there was no blemish in him'. He returns from exile, waits two years, in vain, to be summoned by David. They are finally reunited.

15: Absalom 'stole the hearts of the men of Israel', and summons Ahitophel [Achitophel in the Vulgate], David's counsellor, to aid his conspiracy against the king. David flees Jerusalem, but insists that Zadok the Levite return with the ark. David prays the Lord to 'turn the counsel of Ahitophel into foolishness'. Hushai infiltrates Absalom's retinue.

16: In exile David is cursed by Shimei, who casts stones at David, calling him 'thou man of Belial'.

17: Ahitophel's counsel is overthrown by Hushai's, who persuades Absalom to lead an army in person against David. David receives information via Hushai, and Ahitophel hangs himself.

18: Absalom is defeated in battle and slain despite David's orders to the contrary. David is restored but laments: 'O my son Absalom, my son, my son Absalom! would God I had died for thee, O Absalom, my son, my son!'

It is evident from this summary that Dryden's allegorical application is not a simple one. There are marked differences between the biblical and the Restoration histories:

(1) Dryden draws upon other parts of the Bible and especially from the great Christian stories of the Temptations of Adam, Eve and Christ, and the Falls of Adam, Eve and Satan.

(2) Dryden does not use all the elements in the biblical story. His David does not flee from his palace; Hushai does not infiltrate the enemy's ranks; Achitophel does not commit suicide; Absalom is not slain. Of course, the fact that the biblical conspirators come to such a bad end acts as a sort of prophecy or warning to Monmouth and Shaftesbury. In this way Dryden partly overcomes the inconvenient incompleteness of Restoration history.

(3) Sometimes parallels have limited application. The most striking is the murder of Amnon which is so prominent in Samuel. In Dryden's poem '*Amnon*'s Murther' (39) is treated ironically, as an example of Absalom's 'warm excesses'. Its biblical application is perfectly clear (it makes perfect sense to regard his deed as 'a Just Revenge for injur'd Fame [reputation]'), but editors have been unable to identify a Restoration Amnon with any certainty.

(4) Achitophel's role is much more prominent in Dryden: he resembles Satan in stature and menace. The Biblical Ahitophel is merely a false counsellor and a tool of Absalom.

(5) In Dryden, David's indulgent attitude to Absalom is given greater stress, but is balanced by the authority of his counterstrokes, which contrast with the biblical David's passivity during the battle. Monmouth's illegitimacy is, in theory, like Absalom's, but in practice it is not an issue in Samuel. The tricky subject of Charles's promiscuity is cleverly circumvented by the biblical parallel: David is the classic example of a king favoured by God despite his misdemeanours and shortcomings.

One way of understanding Dryden's use of allegory is by seeing the stories as running parallel, sometimes one predominating, sometimes the other; sometimes merged and indistinguishable. The poem's brilliant opening is an example of a complete merger: it can be read equally well as biblical or Restoration history. Ultimately, however, the biblical story is true, and, as Earl Miner has said, Restoration history becomes a 'type' of biblical history.

Background

Political allegory was extremely fashionable in seventeenth-century France. Heroic poetry was scrutinized for its hidden political message. The taste for such allegorizing was brought back to England by the court after the Restoration. The use of biblical allegory had been popular with the Puritans in the pre-revolutionary period; they applied the story of Absalom and Achitophel to describe the evil counsellors surrounding the king. During the Civil Wars the allegorized story was used by Roundheads and Cavaliers alike. The restoration of Charles II in 1660 clearly invited comparison with the exile and restoration of the biblical David. In *Astraea Redux* (1660) Dryden described Charles as follows:

> Thus banished David spent abroad his time,
> When to be God's Annointed was his crime...

The perfect moment for a really elaborate parallel between Charles and David came during the Exclusion Crisis, which afforded opportunities for comparisons between Absalom and the disaffected Monmouth, and between Achitophel and the turbulent Shaftesbury. The Achitophel analogy had been used by Parliamentary writers before the appearance of *Absalom* (for example, the Tory prose work, *Absalom's Conspiracy* 1680). Finally, the Catholic John Caryll wrote *Naboth's Vinyard* (1679), which is, like Dryden's poem, a narrative poem in heroic couplets, using a biblical allegory to describe the alleged Popish Plot.

Typology

In typological interpretation of the Bible, Old Testament people and events are regarded as 'types' of those in the New Testament. For example, Adam is a type of Christ, and the manna which fed the Israelites in the wilderness is a type of the host at the communion table instituted by Christ. Typology is a way of reading which treats history as *simultaneous* rather than sequential; everything (past, present and future) connects in a single divine pattern. It is important to note that a 'type' is not a mere shadow which represents something more real. Charles II and Shaftesbury are as real and historical as the reality they connect with. How does this work in Dryden's case? Steven Zwicker has shown that Dryden employs a special use of biblical typology. He says: 'Dryden is showing how events in the sacred history of Israel and England recapitulate the basic terms of the Christian paradigm.' The biblical story of man's Fall and redemption provides an eternal pattern unifying past and present. In this spirit Dryden inserts into the pattern the events immediately preceding 1681 as part of a larger divine plan, which involves the restoration of law and order. As Zwicker says, he uses 'the typological perspective of the Old Testament ... to create an image of the king as divine healer and saviour, and to postulate a "sacred history" of contemporary events'. David becomes a type of Christ, and Absalom a type of Anti-Christ. The English–Israelites are types of the Old Testament elect, who are pampered and prone to go astray. The Puritans are types of the Old Testament zealots.

The political implications of this approach are no less important. Religious dissenters had, especially during the revolutionary part of the century, concentrated their attention on the 'apocalyptic' sections of the Bible (notably the prophecies in the Book of Daniel and Revelation), which stressed the idea of the second coming – a truly new age, not merely a recurrence. Many of the Civil War sects – the Ranters, the Fifth Monarchists, the Diggers, and others – had drawn their revolutionary passion from this strain of prophecy. Dryden's service to the monarchy in counteracting such tendencies was a major one. As George deForest Lord puts it, Dryden worked 'by advancing the conservative myth of restoration against the radical myth of apocalypse'. In *Absalom* Dryden ridicules the apocalyptic thoughts of his predecessors and treats them as the thoughts of a lunatic fringe, cleverly ignoring the masterpieces of such thinking as the poetry of Andrew Marvell (in 'The First Anniversary' on Cromwell).

Masterstudies: Absalom and Architophel

Key to the Allegory

Aaron's race	The priesthood
Abbethdin	A judge (referring to Shaftesbury who was Lord Chancellor, 1672–3)
ABSALOM	THE DUKE OF MONMOUTH
ACHITOPHEL	THE EARL OF SHAFTESBURY
Adriel	The Earl of Mulgrave, a patron of Dryden's
Agag	(?) Lord Stafford, condemned on dates's evidence, 1678
Amiel	Edward Seymour, the Speaker of the House of Commons
Amnon	(?) Sir John Coventry
Annabel	The Countess of Buccleuch (married Monmouth in 1663)
Balaam	The Earl of Huntingdon
BARZILLAI	THE DUKE OF ORMONDE
Bathsheba	The Duchess of Portsmouth
Caleb	(?) The Earl of Essex
CORAH	TITUS OATES
DAVID	CHARLES II
Egypt	France
Egyptian Rites	Roman Catholicism
Gath	Brussels
Hebrew Priests	Anglican clergymen
Hebron	Scotland
Hushai	Laurence Hyde, a patron of Dryden's
Ishbosheth	Richard Cromwell (Oliver's son)
Israel	England
Issachar	Thomas Thynne of Longleat
Jebusites	Roman Catholics
Jerusalem	London
Jewish Rabbins	Anglican theologians
Jews	The English
Jonas	Sir William Jones, the Attorney-General
Jordan's flood	The Irish Channel
Jordan's sand	Dover Beach
JOTHAM	MARQUIS OF HALIFAX (GEORGE SAVILE)
Levites	Dissenting ministers
Michal	Catherine of Braganza, Charles's childless wife

Biblical Allegory and Typology

Nadab	Lord Howard of Escrick
PHARAOH	LOUIS XIV
Sagan	Henry Crompton, Bishop of London
Sandhedrin	Parliament
SAUL	OLIVER CROMWELL
SHIMEI	SLINGSBY BETHEL (Whig Sheriff of London)
Sion	London
Solymæan rout	The London mob (Solyma is another name for Jerusalem)
Tyrus	Holland
Zadoc	William Sancroft, Archbishop of Canterbury
ZIMRI	GEORGE VILLIERS, SECOND DUKE OF BUCKINGHAM

Part II (Lines 310–509 only)

Balak	Gilbert Burnet, later Bishop of Salisbury
BEN-JOCHANAN	SAMUEL JOHNSON
DOEG	ELKANAH SETTLE
Hebron	Scotland
JUDAS	ROBERT FERGUSON, 'the Plotter'
Mephibosheth	Samuel Pordage
OG	THOMAS SHADWELL
PHALEG	JAMES FORBES
Uzza	(?) John How

6 The Heroic Couplet

The heroic couplet imposes constraint, which appeared desirable to many Augustans. Dryden's opinion varied: he sometimes thought the couplet unnatural, corresponding to nothing in real human speech, but at other times he thought it added an aesthetic delight which elevated poetry above mere imitation of speech. In practice, he seems to have followed decorum. The heroic drama, for example, seemed to require the artificial dignity of rhyming couplets on two grounds: first, since drama in general is a special rendering of ordinary life; and second, since the characters of heroic drama are raised even above the usual level. The discipline of the couplet form went with the generally rigorous attitude of neo-classical literary theory towards expression. The ideals of 'correctness' and 'decorum' tended to encourage the regularity of the couplet. In the early phase of Augustan poetry (c. 1650–85), when a poet wished to write more 'enthusiastically', the use of the unruly 'Pindarique' ode was permitted as a way of releasing the poem from strict metrical rules. However, this liberty was far less often entertained after about 1685.

All arts require the discipline of conventions or rules in order to help the beginner to achieve a minimum standard, and to provide a *resistance* against which the artist works to achieve a new effect. Paradoxically, it is more difficult to be fresh and creative when there are no constraints. A blank page and total freedom of action are terribly inhibiting. Sometimes, facile writers believe themselves to be freely and spontaneously creating an individual poetic voice, when in actuality they are slavishly following fashionable models. To achieve total independence from conventions and received models is impossible. To do so would be like being able to speak without ever hearing human speech. On the other hand, one must recognize that some periods are more revolutionary (in all senses) and innovative than others. Even in these cases spontaneity and freedom may not be quite what they appear. William Blake's *Songs of Innocence and Experience* seem totally free from convention and restraint. However, they could not have been written unless Blake had read the Bible and Watts's hymns for children. Not only that, but Blake was operating his own principles of form and contrast. It is true that the period dominated by Dryden produced poetry within a more conservative aesthetic ideology, but still achieved in its best writing a freshness

The Heroic Couplet

and individuality which can be compared with the Romantics and the moderns.

Dryden does not follow the tradition of rough style which survived in the satires of John Oldham. As Walter Scott pointed out: 'he bestowed upon the versification of his satires the same pains which he had given to his rhyming plays and serious poems.' After Dryden 'expression and harmony began to be consulted, in satire, as well as sarcastic humour or powerful illustration'. The 'improvement' of versification was part of the general drive towards 'correctness' which went on in the second half of the century. The neo-classical attitude to the couplet gradually grew stricter under French and classical influence. French versification was strictly syllabic: poets were not at liberty to introduce extra, lightly weighted syllables. English verse has always been freer and more flexible about the deployment of extra syllables. During the Augustan period English poets began to be stricter, in imitation of the French. The line usually had to have ten syllables (except in the rarely admitted 'alexandrine', which had twelve). This meant that all unvoiced syllables were usually (but practice varied) marked as such: 'heav'n', 'e'en' and 'pow'r' are each monosyllabic. 'Th'' and 't'' are non-syllabic versions of 'the' and 'to'. In the line 'The next for Int'rest sought t'embroil the State', a twelve-syllable line is reduced to ten by removing a syllable in 'Interest' (pronounced Int'rest) and another in 'to'. Conversely, in the line 'So over Violent, or over Civil' (557), Dryden requires each syllable to receive its full value, unlike those in 'bubbles o'r' (139). So far, what we have said is hardly inspiring. We have simply noted the rigidity of the basic pattern of the heroic couplet as used by the Augustans. However, the skill of a writer of Dryden's quality is to work with and against the metronome-like beat which the reader's mind supplies. In practice, because stress in English speech is such a complex phenomenon, very few lines have a completely regular alternating stress pattern: $\times\ '\ \times\ '\ \times\ '\ \times\ '\ \times\ '$ ($\times$ = unstressed: $'$ = stressed). The first line to have this regular rhythm is 'Promiscuous use of Concubine and Bride' (6). But even here there are two slight variations: (1) we elide the two syllables at the end of 'Promiscuous'; (2) the last syllable of 'Concubine' is less strongly stressed than the first.

We have already admired the compression and concision of Dryden's verses. He communicates a sense of authoritative judgement through his tightly organized, pithy and often gnomic sentences (a gnomic utterance conveys a general truth in a concentrated and memorable way: 'Great Wits are sure to Madness near ally'd'.). How is this achieved? The main devices which affect metre are:

Masterstudies: Absalom and Achitophel

   (1) antithetical patterning
   (2) alliteration and assonance to reinforce patterning
   (3) stress variation
   (4) pause variation

The portrait of Zimri gives Dryden the opportunity to exploit his couplet technique to the full. Zimri's foolish dogmatism and dilettante approach to life is captured in a tightly organized couplet:

> Stiff in Opinions, always in the wrong;
> Was every thing by starts, and nothing long: (547-8)

Notice how the second half lines compound the follies of the first. To be dogmatic is bad, but to have wrong opinions is worse. To take up too many interests is foolish, but to abandon them quickly is more foolish. The effect is nicely calculated: 'Stiff' is worsened by 'in the wrong'; 'every thing' contrasted with 'nothing', and 'by starts' with 'long'. The lines which convey his dilettantism start with a mixture of roles: 'Chymist, Fidler, States-Man, and Buffoon'. 'Chymist' and 'States-Man' are relatively serious occupations, while 'Fidler' and 'Buffoon' lower the tone which then rapidly deteriorates. Lines 555-8 once more use antithetical patterning:

> Rayling and praising were his usual Theams;
> And both (to shew his Judgment) in Extreams:
> So over Violent, or over Civil,
> That every man, with him, was God or Devil.

'Rayling' (verbal abuse) and 'praising' are both taken to 'Extreams': either too much railing ('over Violent') or too much praise ('over Civil'); either calling a man a 'Devil' or a 'God'.

We will now discuss particular metrical devices. Consider the antithetical patterning in the following lines:

> For him he Suffer'd, and with him Return'd.
> The Court he practis'd, not the Courtier's art:
> Large was his Wealth, but larger was his Heart:
> Which, well the Noblest Objects knew to choose,
> The Fighting Warriour, and Recording Muse. (824-8)

Four of these lines have a 'medial caesura' (a heavy pause often marked by punctuation usually at mid-point in the line). This enables the poet to set up a pattern of echoes, contrasts and antitheses between the two half lines. One can almost imagine the second half of the line being spoken by another voice trying wittily to complement or counterbalance the voice of the first half of the line. 'For him' is balanced by 'with him', 'The

The Heroic Couplet

Court' by 'the Courtier', 'Large' by 'larger'. The word 'him' has the same stressed position in each half line, as do 'Cóurt' and 'Cóurtier'. However, 'Large' and 'larger' are asymmetrical in metrical position: 'Lárge was his Wéalth, but lárger was his Héart'. Each half-line has two main stresses, but if we mark the line according to the regular iambic beat, we see that 'Large' and 'larger' fall in different stress positions: 'Large wás his Wéalth, but lárger wás his Héart'. Not only is there a subtle shift of stress resulting from normal emphases ('Lárge was his' not 'Large wás his', and so on), but the special stress on 'Large' draws attention to Dryden's comparison between Barzillai's 'Wealth' and 'Heart'.

The division of the line encourages a tendency to reduce the number of main stresses. By dropping or de-emphasizing one, the balancing of half-line against half-line is strengthened. The following examples illustrate this point:

> When Náture prómpted, and no láw dený'd (5)
>
> His Fáther gót him with a gréater Gúst (20)
>
> Inclin'd the Bállance to the bétter síde (76)

The de-emphasized syllable is often a preposition or conjunction, as in these cases ('and', 'with' and 'to').

Another kind of variation of stress position goes with the use of 'anaphora' (the repetition of a word or phrase in successive clauses), as in 'Large'/'larger' above. Where the repeated words fall in the same position the effect is of persuasive authority:

> *Secure* his Person to *secure* your Cause;
> They who *possess* the Prince, *possess* the Laws. (475–6)

Even this regularity is only apparent, because the metrical *context* of the repeated words is different in each instance: the second 'secure' follows a de-emphasized 'to', and the first 'possess' follows a stress reversal ('Théy who', not 'They whó'). The following are striking examples of varied stress position:

> *Thee*, Saviour, *Thee*, the Nations Vows confess; (240)
>
> *Still* the same baite, and circumvented *still*! (754)
>
> *How* then *coud* Adam bind his future Race?
> *How coud* his forfeit on mankind take place?
> Or *how coud* heavenly Justice damn us all, (771–3)
>
> Yet *some* there were, ev'n in the worst of days;
> *Some* let me name, and Naming is to praise. (815–16)

Masterstudies: Absalom and Achitophel

> *Law* they require, let *Law* then shew her Face; (1006)

In the following pair of couplets notice how the first and last lines are regular while the second and third disrupt the pattern most effectively:

> The *Law* shall still direct my peacefull Sway,
> And the same *Law* teach Rebels to Obey:
> *Votes* shall no more Establish'd Pow'r control,
> Such *Votes* as make a Part exceed the Whole: (991–4)

The first anaphora ('Law ... Law') repeats the stress position though in a different metrical foot, while the second anaphora ('Votes ... Votes') is in the same foot but in a different stress position. The second line has an irregular stress pattern: × × ′ ′ ′ ′ × × × ′. The third starts with a 'trochaic inversion' (an iambic foot, × ′, is reversed, producing a trochee, ′ ×): 'Votes shall no more' (′ × × ′). Related to these effects is the use of alliteration to underscore balance and antithesis. The stress patterns of some of the most powerful lines are marked in this way:

> To *r*aise up Common-wealths, and *r*uin Kings. (84)
> Of these the *f*alse Achitophel was *f*irst: (150)
> *R*esolv'd to *R*uine or to *R*ule the State. (174)
> *D*rawn to the *d*regs of a *D*emocracy. (227)
> Or gather'd *R*ipe, or *r*ot upon the Tree. (251)

The use of run-on lines can have a strong effect, because so many of the lines are end-stopped that we notice the cases when lines are allowed to flow on. The effects are various. In the following example the enjambement (or run-on) supports the meaning of the clause by expanding its length:

> His vigorous warmth did, variously, impart
> To Wives and Slaves: (8–9)

The emphasis on absence of bounds is similarly reinforced in

> And when no rule, no president was found
> Of men, by Laws less circumscrib'd and bound, (53–4)

A similar effect of breaking boundaries occurs in the following lines:

> And every hostile Humour, which before
> Slept quiet in its Channels, bubbles o'r:
> So, sev'ral Factions from this first Ferment,
> Work up a Foam, and threat the Government. (138–41)

A Miltonic effect of precipitous fall is obtained in lines 273–4:

The Heroic Couplet

> But, like the Prince of Angels from his height,
> Comes tumbling downward with diminish'd light;

Compare Milton's even more dramatic effect:

> With hideous ruin and combustion down
> To bottomless perdition, (*Paradise Lost*, I.46–7).

In his elegiac lines on the Earl of Ossory, Dryden employs a combination of enjambement and the rare 'Alexandrine' with its twelve syllables:

> Now, free from Earth, thy disencumbred Soul
> Mounts up, and leaves behind the Clouds and Starry Pole: (850–1)

'Mounts up' is cunningly lifted up by its position, running on from the previous line and followed by a strong pause and a complete ten syllable line.

Dryden rarely uses extra (hypermetric) syllables in his line, except for special effects. The following passage from the portrait of Zimri illustrates this unusual device and is a good example to conclude our study of versification:

> Stiff in Opinions, always in the wrong;
> Was every thing by starts, and nothing long:
> But, in the course of one revolving Moon,
> Was Chymist, Fidler, States-man, and Buffoon:
> Then all for Women, Painting, Rhiming, Drinking;
> Besides ten thousand freaks that dy'd in thinking.
> Blest Madman, who coud every hour employ,
> With something New to wish, or to enjoy!
> Rayling and praising were his usual Theams;
> And both (to shew his Judgment) in Extreams:
> So over Violent, or over Civil,
> That every man, with him, was God or Devil. (547–58)

The fifth, sixth, eleventh and twelfth lines of the passage all conclude with 'feminine' endings (unstressed final syllables), in each case having eleven syllables instead of ten. The extra energy imparted to the lines emphasizes the manic and lawless vitality of Zimri. This effect is furthered by the repeated crossing of metrical pattern and word division: 'Was Chym-ist, Fid-ler, States-Man' and 'for Wom-en, Paint-ing, Rhim-ing, Drink-ing'. Variety is lent by the three lines having opening trochaic inversions ('Stiff in Opinions', 'But, in the course', 'Rayling and prais-ing'). 'Blest Madman' starts with two stressed syllables which gives emphasis to the phrase. Finally, one should notice the great variety of

Masterstudies: Absalom and Achitophel

pause and caesura in the passage. If we divide the lines by syllables, marking the main pauses, we arrive at the following layout: 5/5 : 6/4 : 1/9 : 10 : 11 : 11 : 3/7 : 6/4 : 5/5 : 2/5/3 : 6/5 : 4/2/5.

The fine detail of metrical analysis may seem tedious, but it reveals the artistry which works by seeming effortless. The Latin motto *ars celare artem* (the art to conceal art) is finely illustrated in Dryden's prosody.

Bibliography

Editions

The Poems of John Dryden, ed. James Kinsley, 4 vols (1958)
The Works of John Dryden (The California Dryden), ed. E. N. Hooker, H. T. Swedenberg, and others (University of California Press, 1956–). *Absalom and Achitophel* is in vol. 2 (1972)
Absalom and Achitophel and Other Poems, ed. Philip Roberts (Collins, 1973)

Dryden's intellectual background

Bredvold, L. I., *The Intellectual Milieu of Dryden's Thought* (University of Michigan Press, 1934)
Harth, Phillip, *Contexts of Dryden's Thought* (University of Chicago Press, 1968). Supersedes Bredvold in some respects

Dryden's poetry and especially *Absalom and Achitophel*

Jack, Ian, *Augustan Satire*, pp. 52–76 (Clarendon Press, 1952)
Lord, George deForest, '"Absalom and Achitophel" and Dryden's Political Cosmos,' in *Writers and Their Background: John Dryden*, (ed. Earl Miner), pp. 156–90 (G. Bell & Sons, 1972)
Miner, Earl, *Dryden's Poetry*, chapter 4: 'Metaphorical History: *Absalom and Achitophel*' (Indiana University Press, 1967)
Myers, William, *Dryden*, chapter 5: 'The Exclusion Crisis: Poems, plays and satires, 1679–1681' (Hutchinson, 1973)
Rivers, Isabel, *The Poetry of Conservatism 1600–1745*, Chapter 4: 'John Dryden: The Recreation of Monarchy' (Rivers Press, 1973)
Schilling, Bernard N., *Dryden and the Conservative Myth: A Reading of Absalom and Achitophel* (Yale University Press, 1961)
Selden, Raman, *English Verse Satire 1590–1765*, chapter 4 (Allen & Unwin, 1978)
Swedenberg, H. T. (ed.), *Essential Articles for the Study of John Dryden*, Articles by R. F. Jones and Godfrey Davies (Archon Books, 1966)
Thomas, W. K., *The Crafting of Absalom and Achitophel: Dryden's 'Pen For a Party'* (Waterloo, Ontario, Wilfred Laurier University Press, 1978)
Van Doren, Mark, *John Dryden. A Study of his Poetry* (Harcourt, Brace, 1920). Still a useful overview of Dryden's literary career
Vieth, D. M., 'The Discovery of the Date of *Mac Flecknoe*', in *Evidence in Literary Scholarship*, eds. R. Wellek and A. Ribeiro (Clarendon Press, 1979)

Masterstudies: Absalom and Achitophel

Wykes, David, *A Preface to Dryden* (Longman, 1977)
Zwicker, Steven N., *Dryden's Political Poetry*, pp. 88–104 (Brown University Press, 1972)

Books on the seventeenth century

Feiling, K. G., *A History of the Tory Party, 1640–1714* (Clarendon Press, 1924; 1951)
Haller, William, *The Rise of Puritanism* (1938)
Hill, Christopher, *The Century of Revolution 1603–1714* (Thomas Nelson, 1961)
——, *Change and Continuity in Seventeenth-Century England* especially chapter 8: 'The Many-Headed Monster' (Weidenfeld and Nicolson, 1974)
Kenyon, J. P., *The Popish Plot* (1972, Penguin, 1974)
——, *Stuart England* (Penguin, 1978). Reliable short account of the seventeenth century
Nevo, Ruth, *The Dial of Virtue: A Study of Poems on Affairs of State in the Seventeenth Century* (Princetown University Press, 1963)
Ogg, David, *England in the Reign of Charles II*, second edition (Oxford, Oxford University Press, 1956)
Tawney, R. H., *Religion and the Rise of Capitalism* (1926, Penguin, 1938)
Thirsk, Joan, *The Restoration*. A useful anthology of material, especially on religion, politics and economics (includes extracts from the work of Christopher Hill, Lipson, and others)
Webster, Charles, ed., *Past and Present: The Intellectual Revolution of the Seventeenth Century* (1974)